Electronic communication in construction

Tim Cole

Thomas Telford

Published by Thomas Telford Publishing, Thomas Telford Ltd, 1 Heron Quay, London E14 4JD
URL: http://www.t-telford.co.uk

Distributors for Thomas Telford books are
USA: ASCE Press, 1801 Alexander Bell Drive, Reston, VA 20191-4400
Japan: Maruzen Co. Ltd, Book Department, 3-10 Nihonbashi 2-chome, Chuo-ku, Tokyo 103
Australia: DA Books and Journals, 648 Whitehorse Road, Mitcham 3132, Victoria

First published 2000

A catalogue record for this book is available from the British Library

ISBN: 0 7277 2746 X

Typeset by Pier Publishing, Brighton
Printed and bound in Great Britain by Bell & Bain, Glasgow

Preface

Although this book may be about electronic information exchange with a focus on the construction sector, much of what is contained here could apply to any change process in any industry.

Commercial, economic and social factors have all played their part in a saga that has cost the construction industry millions of pounds and which has inhibited much needed process re-engineering.

We embraced the computer and enjoyed the benefits it offered in maintaining and controlling increasingly complex operations. What we failed to avoid was the barrier this created to subsequent process integration, especially between the different organizations collaborating on a construction project.

To prevent any confusion I would like to make it clear that this is neither a veiled attack on computers, nor a vote for traditional processes. It is precisely because of the growth of computerized processing capabilities that the opportunity to streamline and integrate operations has come about. The difficulty lies in achieving that potential. This is also not another drive for the paperless office – I find paper much easier to read than a computer terminal. It is about recognizing that paper is not a sensible import medium for computer applications.

With traditional paper-based project management, information was indeed integrated between the client, architect, engineers, surveyors, contractors and suppliers to the level that could be achieved given the imposed time and cost constraints. This required each party to take responsibility for completing work largely in isolation but in a way that could then be coordinated with the others. As with all tasks, we gradually perfected the art and became familiar with our part in the play.

At some time during the late 1980s, probably in the mid-1990s for most, it became apparent that computers had become widely accepted as the way to run an efficient construction operation. From computer-aided design (CAD) and estimating, to project management and procurement, organizations were gaining from improved information management.

What happened next remains a mystery. Some say we were all busy coming out of another recession, others that we were too excited playing the latest version of computer golf (before the boss banned it and took it home again!), but none of us managed to prevent Old Father Time winding back the clock. Mind you, it was subtly done! All our computers continued to work (most of the time) and we got faster and smarter at lots and lots of really worthwhile things. What Old Father Time had done was to let us forget the importance of communicating with each other.

Before we had computers we exchanged written information on paper and transferred it by post. With computers, we learnt how to produce information faster and in greater quantities, but we rarely upgraded our communication capabilities. Our ability to exchange information between systems remained paper based and had become a limiting factor.

As an industry we had soon purchased a plethora of powerful operating systems that, integration wise, made the Tower of Babel look like a well organized international conference.

Now we have to rebuild communications appropriate to the operational capabilities of the applications upon which we are increasingly reliant – only now we have to do it on the run.

The benefits that flow from integrated information are, to use an overworked generalization, 'considerable'. Add to this the almost universal agreement that, as an industry, we must achieve effective information exchange, and you are left wondering why this was not adopted years ago. 'Surely it cannot be that good, or we would all be doing it?' Well, before we become too analytical about this, let's face it, we all know that regular exercise and a healthy diet is good for us too, but the world is not full of decathletes. What more and more organizations are realizing is that electronic information exchange is easier to achieve than many believed and that the benefits are genuinely worth the effort. Add to this the risk to business competitiveness from an inappropriate delay to adopt new practices and the analogy is complete. Mmmm, perhaps I'll try that salad after all.

Contents

1

What is electronic information exchange?

> **Let's be clear from the start!**
>
> Electronic information exchange (EIE) is a term that I will use to cover the whole spectrum of business applications that involve the transfer of information electronically between computer systems.

1.1 EDI, EIE, the Internet, the WWW, electronic commerce, e-business ... and all that!

I have increasingly used the term 'EIE' to overcome the denigration of the term 'electronic data interchange' (EDI) that has occurred over recent years. This denigration has been caused primarily by those seeking to define the Internet-based developments as being distinct from established practices. EDI has been around for over two decades and remains a broad definition covering the exchange of information between different computer systems without the need for manual re-keying. At its heart lie data format definitions that allow information to be compressed for ease of transport between trading partners. Therefore, these formats invariably have to be converted (mapped) before they can be displayed by the receiving application. It is at this level that the distinction in terminology has been made.

The Internet, with the World Wide Web (WWW or Web), has provided a global information platform. The Internet is correctly defined as an 'information superhighway', whereas the WWW was initially a display-based interface that used the Internet to link users and information sites. The growth of the WWW has innevitably led to an increase in its role to support data transfer services. Its visual interface clearly overcomes the poor interface characteristics of EDI. However, visualization is something that people do. Computers are more reliant on strict data rules than pictures if they are to communicate with each other.

Understanding this difference between how people and computers best interface with information should help us to understand why different terminologies have arise; for example:

- EDI iss definitely about computer to computer exchange
- electronic commerce (or e-commerce) brought in new opportunities, such as Internet shopping, where people could, for example, interface with someone else's computer from almost anywhere in the world
- e-business is an extension of e-commerce which takes in the whole business process such as linking an electronic order system to warehousing and despatch operations
- the WWW makes the Internet accessible and more visually attractive
- the Internet is the global information-transfer network at the heart of the WWW
- EIE as used in this book combines EDI with the new exchange opportunities of the Internet, WWW, etc.

The value of computer to computer exchange combined with the global nature of the Internet has inevitably led to a new range of information services. Application protocols allow software to run on WWW integrated computers, and now we have a new Internet data language (XML, or extensible markup language). XML supports the exchange of computer displayable documents in a fully structured format and is a subject I will return to later in the book. Interestingly, the established EDI data formats have often been used to provide the rules required to enable computer to computer exchange in the XML format.

This combination of the 'established' and the 'new' underlines the folly of terminology-based distinctions and the importance of retaining a clear business perspective. EIE encompasses EDI, XML and anything else that helps us to integrate our computers as easily as we can integrate people within a project team.

1.2 Did it help that EDI became a rude word?

Would you believe it! Just as most business managers had come to understand the term EDI, along came this whole wave of fashionable terminology. Should we be implementing EDI, or e-commerce, or Internet commerce … or just waiting until someone sorts it out once and for all?

The English language is occasionally stripped of a word when common usage corrupts its original meaning. Words have to be used with caution, as to some they can portray quite a different meaning to that intended. That 'wicked' to many people now means 'really good' is just one such example, and context does not provide many clues. A child that says 'my teacher is really wicked' could cause alarm to an unsuspecting adult, not to mention a likely disturbance at the parents' evening. The child's true intention was only to acclaim the ability of the teacher – though the particular ability possessed by the Teacher is not clear! And so it seems to be with the term EDI. The name has not changed, but the perception of its meaning clearly has.

With the emergence of the Internet and new data exchange opportunities, many have decided that EDI must mean 'old hat'. It is perverse that people in the construction industry came to besmirch the name of a technology that most had lauded for the best part of a decade, whilst failing to exploit its potential.

Consultants selling the latest Internet offering have often used the damning prefix 'traditional' when referring to EDI. This status is bestowed to set it in a historical context and can be dangerously misleading. Two people could refer to 'EDI' in a conversation, completely unaware that one of them sees it as an embrasive term covering all structured data exchange (including the latest Internet services) whilst the other believes the reference is to a particular, slightly out of date, form of information exchange. To my mind, the latter of these two people is wrong on several counts, but frankly such a view is irrelevant. Fighting such a battle would only lead to a Pyrrhic victory. The matter at stake is the effectiveness of an industry, not the name we should give to a specific process.

To put the record straight, EDI is:

> the exchange of any structured data
>> from one application to another application
>>> avoiding the re-keying of data
>>>> using standardized formats and
>>>>> which is system and hardware independent.

In other words, EDI is a general term that covers tried and tested technologies as well as the Internet and all that is yet to come.

For those of you implementing electronic exchange, I suggest that unless the term EDI is qualified, its use should be avoided. This is why I have adopted the term electronic information exchange (EIE) as a suitable alternative. EIE covers the breadth of this subject and should prevent anyone trying to pigeon-hole your ideas based only on a misinterpretation of your acronym.

On a point of principle I shall probably continue to fight for a Pyrrhic campaign medal, but only over coffee and with people who annoy me by referring to EDI as being 'traditional'! The industry has spent too much time on terminology and not nearly enough on practice. We need to shift the balance. In time, the name will matter no more than does PSTN to my mother every time she picks up the phone and calls me for a chat. Acronyms never get in her way!

1.3 Building on solid foundations

Anything 'new' tends to grab our attention. The danger is that we get drawn in by the opportunities and can lose sight of how these are to be achieved. Reinventing the proverbial wheel can follow where knowledge of the 'established' (to some redundant) technology is not exploited. Given that the construction industry has started to implement EIE at a time when the 'established' and the 'new' technologies are vying for their rightful place in the equation, an understanding of the basic principle is a good place to start. From this perspective we can see how the Internet has added to the picture and opened new horizons in addition to established opportunities.

Just as people communicate with each other through the spoken word, so computers interface best by exchanging data. That we have traditionally made them print everything out for someone to type back in again is the very essence of the opportunity outlined in this book (positive slant intended). Paper is a valuable business medium for use by warm-blooded individuals who have every reason to argue the merits of traditional ways to receive our daily dose of information. But, using paper for data transfer between inanimate computers is undoubtedly a waste of the skills afforded by the computer and its human operator.

Modern living increasingly brings us into contact with ever more sophisticated computer applications, ranging from the Internet to handling the increasingly pervasive range of voice-mail systems found in modern business life. We can even book holidays and order products on the Web, but this is not all EIE. EIE is about how information is exchanged directly between one computer application and another

Figure 1.1 Information transfer from my computer to yours

(*Figure 1.1*). It may, or may not, use the Internet, but will certainly involve information passing from one computer to another. Therefore, typing data into a form on a Web site (even if it is on the other side of the world) is not EIE. However, if you were able to download the data content of the form and then load the resultant file into a program on your computer, that would be EIE.

Another example of EIE would be sending electronic invoices to your customers. The supplier could have delivered 150 lorry loads of its product in the month to a processing plant, each of which generates an invoice. To print out and post 150 invoices incurs costs for the supplier and requires the customer to process each document manually by keying the data into their accounts system. The use of EIE would be to define a format (data exchange standard) for the invoice data so that this can be sent to the customer as a data file. This file can then be loaded directly into the customer's accounts system within seconds and with confidence in the data accuracy.

The scope for EIE is almost limitless and the characteristics (see *Box 1.1*) cover many different exchange scenarios. As I have said, some commentators have defined Internet exchange as being distinct from pre-existing forms of electronic exchange. Surely, arguments that appear to distinguish one type of electronic exchange as being better than another is like suggesting that French is a better language than Italian or that hand-written letters are better than those from a word processor. They are different and will each work best in a particular set of circumstances. But they all come under the general classification of human communications. Likewise, EIE will come in many guises but will always be about how to pass information effectively from one application to another.

Managers should remain focused on matters such as commercial gains and supply chain partnering, and not focus on which exchange protocol was used or which route the data took in reaching its destination. For this reason, I take the broadest possible definition so as to retain the primary focus on the business objectives.

1.4 Accepting our differences

Most of us find it frustrating to be presented with a computerized switchboard that proceeds to fire questions at us, asking us to respond by pressing the buttons on the keypad. I would certainly prefer to speak with someone directly as the spoken word is a form of communication with which I am very familiar. To a computer, life is much easier. Computers never get frustrated – they either work, or they

---

Box 1.1 The characteristics of EIE

Any structured data
    that is exchanged from ...
one computer application to another
    without ...
manual re-keying of data
    (hopefully) using a ...
standardized data format
    which is ...
independent of the operating system and hardware

---

don't. Should we want to enter data via the keypad we won't hear them 'tut tutting' under their breath, and neither will they say 'thanks, I much prefer my data that way' should we present them with a data file. The choice as to how we effectively exchange information between computer applications is down to us.

EIE should be used when no value is added by presenting paper-based information that is to be re-keyed into another computer application. We may also need a paper copy, but if we want the data entered into our computer this should at least be given equal consideration. After all, the receiving application could print out a copy, possibly to our own standard layout specification rather than the multitude of formats used by our trading partners.

There are many definitions of what I call EIE that have been put forward over recent years, though most amount to the same thing. Given the recent growth of electronic information exchange, boosted significantly by the growth of Internet-based exchange, there is little value in considering the semantics of one definition over another. The definition in the following box is one that I have used and which I put into context by defining the opportunity at the same time.

Definition of EIE
The electronic transfer of data between the independent computer systems of business partners, using agreed standards to structure the data

The opportunity
The simple and accurate exchange of business documents with trading partners, regardless of the computer systems being used

---

1.5 Data exchange standards for EIE

When computers became an everyday part of business life, it was not long before consideration was given to how information should be effectively exchanged from one application to another. Initially, the use of computers was not widespread and therefore global solutions were not sought from the outset. Mankind may wish that it was possible to go back to the time before the Tower of Babel and ensure a common basis for the exchange of the spoken word but, sadly, this is not possible. To many people, the cultural value from a diversity of spoken languages and dialects provides a considerable attraction. Despite a personal weakness in foreign-language skills, I see merit in this argument. Be that as it may, to extend this principle to support multiple data languages for computer to computer communications is much harder to sustain.

The idea of a data exchange standard is to provide a common format that software developers can write to, or read from, which can be used by other software products (*Figure 1.2*). Such standards deliver the greatest value where there are many companies involved in the exchange, and there are many different software products needing to exchange information. Groups of trading companies, business sectors, and even whole countries have developed data exchange standards to provide for their particular needs. For example, the automotive industry has the ODETTE standard, the Americans have the ANSI X12 standard and the UK has developed the Tradacoms standard.

It was not long before organizations using different data exchange standards wished to exchange information between themselves. Either one party had to support both standards or progress was halted. Providing multiple interfaces for each different data standard adds significantly to the set-up costs. This cost creates an understandable barrier to the widespread adoption of electronic exchange. Thus, as computers became an intrinsic part of the overall process, the need for an international exchange standard became equally apparent

So it was, under the United Nations International Organization for Standardization (ISO), that international data exchange standards came into force. These standards were to be known as the UN/EDIFACT standards. For reasons perhaps only ever to be known by those in the EDIFACT community, EDIFACT stands for 'electronic data interchange for administration commerce and transport'. This is another bit of jargon that business managers can happily ignore. In practical terms, the emergence of EDIFACT meant that there would

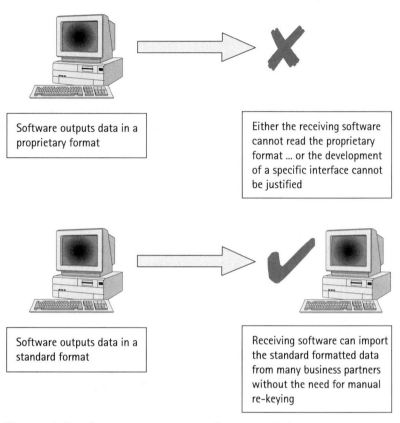

Figure 1.2 Proprietary versus common exchange standards

be an international format for the electronic transfer of business documents.

New electronic exchange developments were quickly able to take advantage of the well-defined and increasingly comprehensive range of standards provided by EDIFACT. However, there were still sizeable communities using the national- or sector-based standards which, it is anticipated, will continue to operate for some years.

Construction activity knows no bounds and crosses readily between industry sectors and over international boarders. Thus, being late into the world of electronic information exchange, enabled the contract companies quickly to identify the value of using the internationally based EDIFACT standards. One of the problems associated with the construction industry being slower to adopt EIE than other sectors (retail, engineering, etc.) was that a number of builders merchants and suppliers of building materials had become users of the Tradacoms standard in response to the commercial requirements of DIY stores, etc. Fortunately this does not appear to have delayed progress, as many of those that had established exchange using the Tradacoms standard have been able to migrate to use the EDIFACT standards as well.

The decision by the construction industry to use the EDIFACT standards has been strengthened by the adoption of EDIFACT formats by the Inland Revenue and the banking world to underpin their own EIE developments. Internet exchange standards, such as extensible markup language (XML), are also utilizing the structure and business rules of EDIFACT. This link between EDIFACT and the Internet-based XML language underlines the validity of the general term EIE. XML is a key tool in the extension of EIE across the Internet and is now one of the fundamental data exchange standards. This is covered later in this book, but already the construction industry is embracing XML alongside proprietary and EDIFACT standards to ensure the right solution is delivered to meet each exchange opportunity.

1.6 Making a connection

> When linking your computers to the outside world, think of the interface as a 13 amp plug and try to avoid it becoming like the tangle of wires behind many hi-fi systems!

Making a connection between your computer and someone else's, especially the first time, can be fraught with all kinds of unnecessary difficulties for the uninitiated. I say 'unnecessary' in the same way that

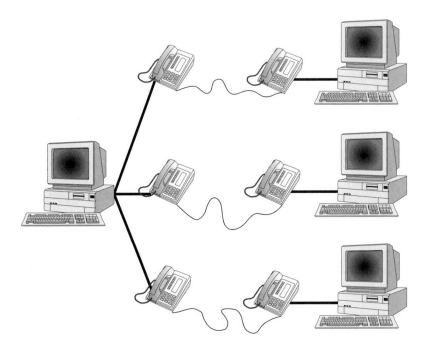

Figure 1.3 Multiple phone interfaces

problems erecting flat-packed furniture are unnecessary, though they are experienced all too often.

During the early days for of EIE, trading partners would agree to establish a link between their computer systems. IT professionals from both companies would liaise to agree the data format and business rules to enable the exchange to be achieved. Pragmatism would often result in a bespoke format being adopted, although increasingly exchange standards became available. In spite of the emergence of these standards, many systems gradually become adorned with multiple interfaces. Though unseen, this is just the same as if we added a new telephone to our desk each time we gained a new trading partner (*Figures 1.3* and *1.4*). Had the multiple data exchange links been as visible as a desk covered by dozens of telephones, I believe the insistence on adopting an international standard would have been pursued more actively.

When establishing an exchange link, the first priority will be to achieve the agreed commercial benefits from trading electronically. Priority two should be to seek the most cost-effective and future-proof implementation. This means enabling multiple electronic trading partnerships to be achieved using the one exchange standard (*Figure 1.5*). More specifically, you should adopt the one exchange standard that offers you access to the largest number of your key trading partners.

Despite general moves to migrate towards international standards, the historical use of the UK-only data format (Tradacoms), for example, makes it likely that many companies will face the question of which standard to adopt ... or whether they may even have to use

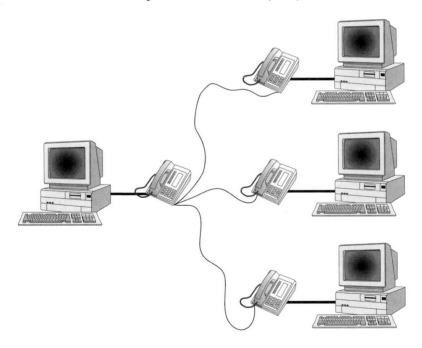

Figure 1.4 Single phone interface

several! Experience in the construction industry has shown that established EIE users are often prepared to adopt the international exchange standards where the longer term benefits of such a move can be identified. Specifically, this has led to companies already using Tradacoms adopting the international EDIFACT standard. Be prepared to ask, even when the request comes from one of your customers.

1.7 The CITE initiative

CITE, which stands for the 'construction industry trading electronically', is a collaborative electronic data exchange initiative for the UK

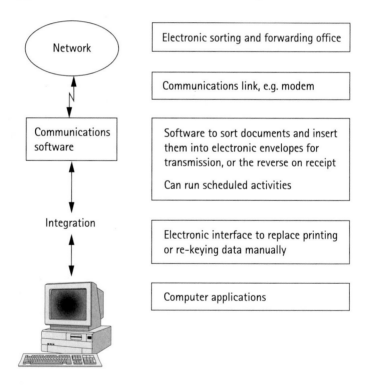

Figure 1.5 The elements of EIE (application to/from a network)

construction industry. The initiative was launched in April 1995, which formally marked the start of a major collaborative undertaking. Building on international standards wherever appropriate, the CITE initiative was established to 'make electronic information exchange happen'. CITE is owned and run by the organizations that make up its membership. Government funding supported initial activities, but the real drive came from contractors, suppliers and professional services who identified the value of adopting a common approach to delivering a common information exchange solution.

It was recognized that many set-up costs would be duplicated and so practical implementation services were provided alongside the technical data exchange formats. It was also recognized that businesses of all sizes needed to be able to become involved. During 1999, CITE combined activities to incorporate those of the EDICON (EDI in construction) organization. EDICON had similar objectives and predated CITE by several years. CITE had taken on the mantle of implementation, while EDICON retained links with international standards bodies and covered the broader range of strategic exchange developments. It was rightly decided that the industry needed one clear voice and so both agreed to combine strengths under a single banner.

1.7.1 Mission and goal

The mission statement for the combined organization is:

> To make electronic information exchange happen in the construction industry by promoting awareness, encouraging collaboration, providing industry representation and developing exchange standards.

The goal is:

> To achieve industry-wide operational benefits through the implementation of electronic information exchange.

1.7.2 CITE information exchange standards

For EIE to become a reality for the construction sector, exchange standards will be required to underpin application developments. Many of the problems experienced with earlier exchange initiatives, primarily outside the construction industry, were as a result of company centred initiatives. The cost of establishing data exchange was therefore higher and the scope limited to perhaps a few trading partners. Through the CITE initiative, the set-up costs are lower and the scope far, far greater. CITE exchange standards provide the opportunity for a establishing a global trading community.

CITE standards have reflected the acceleration of exchange technology and include EDIFACT, XML and proprietary (i.e. pragmatic) options. All CITE standards can be exchanged across the Internet, though it is expected that the EDIFACT option will be used for some time to come for bulk, or repetitive, trading messages (invoices, orders, etc.), as in other industries.

Within the first three years, CITE provided over a dozen data exchange standards:

- enquiries
- quotations
- orders
- despatch advice
- packing list
- invoice
- credit notes
- tenders
- valuations
- goods receipt note automation
- project information
- product, price and availability
- Internet and data exchange.

1.7.3 CITE project activities

The CITE initiative operates by delivering specific exchange solutions that are developed through collaboration between the different organizations involved in each process. These project teams are known as 'subgroups' and they have been the powerhouse behind the initiative. The impact of collaboration on delivering solutions to the industry cannot be overstated. These groups bring together a considerable amount of expertise and the determination to implement the fruits of their labours. The following summarizes just some of these activities.

Bill of quantities (BoQ)/valuations subgroup

When CITE was first established, the importance of electronic tendering was clearly identified. Information that will be used throughout the life of a project should be exchanged electronically from the outset. The BoQ and valuations exchange standards were therefore developed by a project group drawing on the support of contractors, cost consultants and software providers. The standards are now established, but the group continues to meet to support and extend their application. Importantly, operational use was soon achieved, though this flagged up plenty of new issues to be resolved before a final standard was delivered to the industry.

Trading subgroup

The trading group has delivered the largest number of CITE standards (including enquiry, quotation, order, despatch advice and invoice message standards) building on international exchange opportunities. This group brings together contractors, suppliers and software providers and also supports the development of the essential integration services (data conversion and software support) that link software applications to the exchange standards.

Within the trading subgroup project sits a related activity looking at the effective use of purchase cards. This project is looking to increase the effectiveness of purchase cards in construction as part of a comprehensive electronic trading environment. Electronic orders and invoices will be effected by the use of purchase cards. Indeed, the

CITE orders standard allows the sender to include authorization details so that payment can be made using their purchase card. The commercial value available from the use of purchase cards will increase further when transaction data can be conveyed electronically from the point of sale through to an electronic card statement.

Project information exchange (PIX)

This project group has been responsible for defining and implementing a single standard that will embrace a potentially endless number of contract critical documentation. The PIX standard covers the exchange of project documents ranging from technical queries to architects instructions, final certificates and beyond. This standard is built around Internet exchange and could become one of the most widely used CITE standards.

Automation of goods receipt (GRN group)

Lost delivery notes and payment delays caused by 'proof of delivery' disputes are just two reasons for automating the exchange of delivery information. Achieving greater visibility and confidence at the point of delivery is the key to redefining the order, delivery and payment process. Different operational practices can then be implemented to suit specific business requirements.

Building on the trading standards (orders, despatch notes, invoices, etc.), this project looked to re-engineer the goods-receipt process on construction sites to provide an integrated procurement process. The first implementation used a simple, but highly accessible, bar-coded despatch note number as the key to data integration. Already different contractors have demonstrated how a simple 'data key' can unlock many benefits, not least of which is the reduction of delivery based payment disputes. Future developments will undoubtedly use new data transfer technologies (smart cards, memory tags, etc.) to extend these benefits.

With effective data exchange at the order and delivery stages, subsequent administration can clearly be reduced. This group, working closely with the trading group, also considered how improved process viability at the supply stage can build trust so that redundant document exchange can be removed from the process. For example, the despatch note, invoice and statement all say much the same thing and generate considerable administration costs for both parties. Are all still needed when it is known that data were successfully transferred in the first message?

Product information exchange

This is a major undertaking, working towards a common exchange format for product, price and availability information. The scope of this undertaking covers the complete construction process. This group has also identified the growing role that will be played by the WWW in exchanging product information. As a result, the standard is being built using the established data and business rules provided by EDIFACT to create an effective XML standard. The group is also working in close liaison with those developing the 'object' definitions that are increasingly bringing construction products to life, as well as the international aecXML project ('aec', architecture, engineering and construction). An object definition (e.g. 'This object is a blue door on this side and has these relations to the things around it') can be used from the design stage through to procurement and maintenance requirements beyond.

Internet and data standards

Pragmatic standards have been set by this group to encourage better use of the Internet and other data exchange services. Commercial information providers have looked to the industry to set out agreed rules in guiding electronic data services. CITE is seen as the organization responsible for electronic data standards and so has initiated a process to establish workable guidelines.

Inland Revenue – construction industry scheme (electronic lodgement of subcontractor tax information)

During 1999 the Inland Revenue launched a new scheme for the management of tax information relating to payments made to sub-contractors. As part of this scheme, contractors are able to submit payment records electronically, using EDIFACT-based standards. CITE played an important role in coordinating the industry's objectives relating to this scheme and in providing a cost-effective implementation route for contractors.

1.7.4 Supporting implementation

CITE members can, and do, take advantage of a growing range of targeted support services to help them gain the maximum benefits from electronic exchange. These include:

- *Help desk.* This provides independent support and advice to help build confidence to enable companies to proceed, and help to avoid unnecessary expense or delay.
- *Training.* A range of options are provided to raise awareness, empower managers and exploit the full potential of electronic exchange.
- *Implementation support.* From training to 'data mapping' (the conversion of data from one layout to another), which was predicted to save each company many thousands of pounds compared with the traditional implementation costs for each document to be exchanged.
- *Software accreditation scheme.* The objective is to build confidence and promote implementation of electronic exchange. This was established to allow CITE members quickly to ascertain the capabilities of software. It also supported the service providers that implemented the CITE exchange formats within their products.

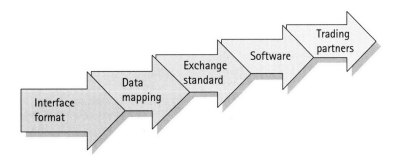

Figure 1.6 Nearly a turn-key solution

1.7.5 Involving the service providers

The strong centralized approach delivered by CITE garnered the support of a growing number of software providers. Software companies were keen to promote the use of computer applications and the effective exchange of data between them. CITE enabled software providers to buy into a solution that promoted the greater take-up (and effective use) of their products.

Fragmentation, bespoke solutions, inertia and high set-up costs were all obstacles to process improvement that the industry sought to avoid by establishing CITE and driving forward implementation within commercial operating systems:

- By providing a strong centralized initiative for the industry, CITE has garnered the support of a growing number of service providers in promoting and implementing common standards.
- Fragmentation, bespoke solutions, inertia and high set-up costs have all been avoided by establishing CITE and driving forward implementation within commercial operating systems.
- CITE has allowed software providers to buy into a solution that promotes greater take-up of their products while delivering the practical support essential to CITE's objective of 'making EIE happen' (*Figure 1.6*).

Thanks to the support of the commercial software companies, solutions are becoming increasingly 'off the shelf'. Application centred exchange services mean that companies can start trading electronically, whether they have previous experience of electronic exchange or not.

1.7.6 Four steps to EIE

Step 1: be aware

EIE changes the nature of business operations – *for the better*. However, those unaware of how it should be deployed can make costly mistakes when setting up their early exchange links. Such mistakes can easily be avoided where managers understand the simple, yet powerful, principles of EIE.

Step 2: be involved

From a commercial perspective, knowing that something is as inevitable as EIE, but not being involved, can be extremely dangerous. The early implementers will gain an understanding of the technology and how it can best be exploited. CITE provides a universal platform for the fast and cost-effective expansion of your electronic partnering initiatives. Software providers, contractors, suppliers, professional services and others have collaborated to drive forward change. By being actively involved in CITE you open the door on a whole new world of commercial opportunities to reduce waste and add value to your business.

Step 3: implementation

Use CITE to build your operational exchange links. All companies that have started to exchange electronic information using CITE have wanted to find *more* trading partners and none has ever looked to return to traditional exchange.

Step 4: exploitation

Having implemented EIE, the innovation process inherent in all companies should be brought to bear on how processes can be redesigned as a result. EIE should lead to a controlled revolution across the spectrum of commercial operations as redundancy is removed and value is added to the global process. The benefits of integration flow across the whole process. Those who build improvements only into their own piece of the jigsaw will fail to grasp the full significance of this revolution.

1.8 Other initiatives

I feel a bit like the actor who wins an award and uses the acceptance speech to mention everyone from his mother to the pet dog who have been instrumental in his success. Setting off for the full list is almost certainly going to lead to one or two being left out, not to mention the boredom this reigns on the audience. Alternatively, you mention just a few key people and hope your brevity is at least respectful. Here I shall go for the latter approach. The one activity missing from this list is the EDICON initiative. If only to give you something to look forward to, I felt it was more appropriate to include EDICON in Chapter 3.

1.8.1 MERNET

This is an electronic trading initiative established by the Builders' Merchants Federation (BMF). The aim was to help its members, their suppliers and customers to benefit from electronic trading. To help achieve this objective, MERNET provided a packaged approach that combined exchange standards, communications software, a network connection, training and awareness services. MERNET predates CITE and probably delivered some of the first operational EDI implementations in the construction industry. This also meant that companies used the UK Tradacoms standard though EDIFACT options are also supports. Liaison with CITE and EDICON included awareness raising at conference events and one joint message development. It is clearly important for builders' merchants to be included.

1.8.2 The International Alliance for Interoperability (IAI)

The IAI, apart from being hard to say, is an international construction industry initiative to define object definitions or data templates that can be exchanged between different applications. Such applications could be as diverse as computer aided design (CAD), procurement or specification systems. Clearly, exchanging information between CAD different packages without losing any of the detail is one opportunity, though anyone involved in the IAI would soon point out that there is much more to the IAI. The aim was to redefine the way an object, such as a window or door, is represented and to do so in a way that allows additional attributes to be included as required. A link established with the CITE initiative recognized the clear association between the object definitions and the need to transfer these within the range of electronic business messages. (Further information about the IAI is included in Appendix 5.)

1.8.3 eCentre^{uk}

Having been formed by the merger of the Electronic Commerce Association (ECA) and the Article Number Association (ANA), eCentre^{uk} is a national body supporting electronic commerce developments.

The construction industry, through the CITE and EDICON organizations, has liaised closely with eCentre^{uk} to maintain a coherent approach to both the industry and global aspects of electronic commerce. Whereas the exchange of tender documents or architects' instructions, for example, have a specific industry application, legal and banking issues will clearly impact across all sectors. The two-way exchange of ideas and practical support between CITE and eCentre[uk] prevents wheels from being reinvented and gives confidence to those looking to implement electronic exchange within an industry the activities of which spread across industry and national boundaries. (Further information about eCentre[uk] is included in Appendix 1.)

2

From a business perspective

My heart raced and my shirt tore as she pulled me into the alley way and the red Mercedes shot past within inches of my face. 'I hope you've got your code list', she yelled at me, as though somehow all this was my fault. I reminded her, with more than a little anger in my voice, that it was she, not I, who had decided against using the international data exchange standard for our purchase invoices, but frankly I was wasting valuable time. Either we were to find the 6411 code element that indicated a truck load of cement or we faced dire consequences. Almost as though scripted by Steven Spielberg, the Mercedes appeared at the other end of the alley-way.

We could only assume that Mike, our Financial Director, had given up on his chances of promotion, having personally backed the electronic information exchange project. Our only hope was to trace the code, reprogram the software interface and register the invoices before he killed us both.

Were the electronic exchange of information that exciting, perhaps more organizations would have raised sufficient interest to have exploited it sooner. The truth is that, from a business effectiveness perspective, electronic information exchange (EIE) is far more exciting – if only you could drag it out of the IT department and set it firmly where it belongs, i.e. on the agenda of your next board or client review meeting. Most importantly, the benefits from system integration, both internally and intercompany, are already available to be applied. The result will undoubtedly redefine business processes in ways that we shall only truly understand when we look back and see how the innovators capitalized fully on this opportunity.

2.1 The real opportunity

What exactly am I talking about? Simply put, 'to discover what part electronic information exchange can play in enabling business managers to achieve their goal'.

2.1.1 But what is our goal?

About ten years ago I was given a book that was simply entitled *The Goal*.[1] It turned out to be a very enjoyable read and a subtle way of forcing me to accept a business principle that all kind hearted people, and I would like to think I am one, seldom like to admit. 'The goal' was to generate cash. It reminded me a little of Maslow's hierarchy of needs,[2] where the basic needs of survival come first and then, but only then, can you start to satisfy other needs leading to personal fulfilment and that wonderful state called 'self-actualization'. If we want to achieve our personal ambitions, however well meaning, we must have created a sound financial basis and planned for its longer term viability.

2.1.2 But the goal-posts keep moving!

Sadly we were not satisfied to stick with the flint axe and became determined to develop better ways of living. Today this quest has delivered the wonders of the computer-based business system.

Despite this notable achievement, human nature continues to drive us forward. We remain dissatisfied with our set of tools and strive for ever greater benefits. As a result, we can't sit back and enjoy what we have, unless at the same time we are planning for what will arrive in the future. We have to look constantly at how progress will impact on our ability to maintain viable operations. The goal moves on. Business managers must be able to judge what needs to be changed as well as when and how to change it.

The questions here are whether construction businesses can remain competitive using traditional communication methods and whether we can afford to keep watching technology advancing without applying these skills to our business. Even the hare eventually found himself too far behind to catch up.

No one would contemplate setting up business operations without installing telephone communication links. Before very long, the same will apply to EIE. This view of life can no longer be described as perceptive. It is an obvious consequence, not to say an essential commercial requirement, following inescapably from the widespread application of computers. Computers don't communicate by post any more than you and I could communicate in binary code. The goal will keep moving, but computers will always be underutilized if we don't start to link them together effectively.

During the late 1980s I witnessed the failure of early attempts to introduce EIE (then referred to as electronic data interchange (EDI)) between trading partners in the construction industry. Over the years I have attended many different seminars and conferences on the same subject. Now, by some twist of fate, I find myself working full time on how to achieve the benefits of EIE within the industry. Progress is being made, and yet inertia still flows, fuelled by the same concerns.

What held us back for so long? What will happen to our businesses as we:

- give up our cherished administration
- extend partnering
- streamline processes?

EIE developments are enabling the construction industry to embark on a process of change that will impact on all business processes. With new technology and commercial pressures both coming to bear on business managers, the need for clear leadership is paramount. The industry needs managers who are aware of the issues and, at the same time, equipped to separate the myths and misinformation from the sound business opportunities. Perhaps it would be fairer to say that 'the goal' has stayed still, but we have kept running around it rather than putting the ball in the back of the net.

2.2 But we are not like that

2.2.1 It takes all sorts to make a world

We are often faced with something new and often this 'something new' does not understand 'us' very well. Rejection of the idea may be an initial reaction on the grounds that it does not readily apply to our situation and such ideas often go away. However, EIE will not go away. The requirement underlining EIE is to work more effectively with the partners involved in the overall project. This may lead to the boundaries of established responsibilities being moved. It might even transform the very composition of the project team. Either way, we must be able to see our role as part of the bigger picture. Progress will be minimal if we only consider how to improve on the delivery of our individual component and are not prepared to support 'through process' benefits. This requires collaboration across borders that may previously have been jealously guarded.

Perhaps like you, I believe that I am unique and, hopefully, the world should be spared from the consequences of this assertion being disproved. This generally healthy perspective should not impair our ability to work within one of the exciting 'teams', or 'virtual teams', that underpin modern corporate life. There is a need to successfully blend our unique talents if we are to achieve the overall team objective. The construction process is probably about as established as an industry can be. Time and time again we have had to adapt to change. Now is just such a time!

2.2.2 The best excuse in the business

Being unique is no bad thing. Believing we are so different that the maxims of business cannot be applied is taking things too far. There is no business like the construction business. Of course, if you look at it on the surface, this may appear to be true. For a start, who else would put up with architects (or is it design consultants?), engineers and quantity surveyors all at the same time! And then there is the repeated starting and stopping of different contracts and the commercial relationships that they bring into effect. These differences are real and significant, but they do not change the basic commercial and logistical forces that apply to all businesses.

I have often been told that the construction industry would have introduced electronic trading sooner if construction was like supplying chicken tikka, or Yum Yums (try them they're delicious!), to Marks and Spencer. The conclusion I am encouraged to draw is that, the construction process bears no similarities to the retail (or most other) sectors of the economy and our 'special condition' condemns us to continuing to plough our established furrow. I can neither recognize, nor accept, this analogy and hope that few would still offer such a defence.

Our basic commercial activities are the same as in any other market sector. Like everyone else, we have clients who need something to be provided at a specified time and for a competitive price. As with a supermarket, where a range of items has to be presented in one place at the right time and at the right price, a construction project is a logistical exercise driven by customer demands. So, not only is construction much like any other commercial undertaking, the fact is that we probably have more to gain from effective communication than most other market sectors.

Construction projects very often take a long time to progress from concept to contract. However, when the starting gun is fired the time available to 'construct the team' is limited. This is not the time to ask whether the various software packages used by the different players can be readily integrated! Project, product and commercial information soon starts to fly around, much as it does at Tescos. We know that we need to be prepared for this before the contract is awarded. We may not even know who our project partners will be, though we do know that there will rarely be time or money allowed in the budget to integrate systems across company boundaries. This either exists, or we will almost certainly have to work without it. When the starting gun has fired, the time for discussing team tactics has passed.

Planning for effective system integration must be completed ahead of time. Each party to the project must know what to expect. Therefore we must have a standardized approach, built into our operating systems, so that expenditure on integration links is not wasted and can be used over and over again – just like Marks and Spencer ordering their stock of Yum Yums.

2.3 What's in it for me?

Everything eventually comes down to money. This is a fact of business life, but quantifying the benefits of EIE either results in a number which is so large that no one believes you, or which is based on so many intangible elements that no one trusts you. This *is* the truth, but it hardly helps make the case for progress.

2.3.1 We just know it's good for us!

How many companies produced a fully justified capital case for the widespread adoption of fax machines? In the vast majority of cases the transition from saying 'our company will never need one' to 'what do you mean you haven't got a fax machine' came upon most of us without our really noticing. Gradually we recognized the inevitable change to the way businesses interfaced with one another and made sure that we maintained our ability to operate effectively and competitively.

So it has been for others, and will be for the construction industry, with EIE. Eventually we shall all be passing data from system to system without re-keying. Eventually we shall have redefined operating procedures, making it impossible to operate effectively without these new communication systems. And eventually we shall no longer talk about whether we can do this or not. Such a capability will be taken for granted and EIE will join the ranks of common usage. After all, it is simply a logical consequence of using computers.

2.3.2 But we can be specific about the benefits

Many of us bought our first fax machine when prices had begun to fall and we had watched others pioneer the practice. The proverbial dove had been sent out and had clearly found dry land. The cost of EIE services is now a fraction of those paid by the pioneers, mainly in other industry sectors, and few, if any, of these 'doves' have returned to the fold disappointed. The same is true for us. The required software that once cost into the tens of thousands can be obtained for your PC for a fraction of the cost and companies that made the first move have only wanted one thing – *more* electronic exchange.

I shall include more detailed case study information later, but the following quick examples show that value can be quantified. It is also true that there are many so-called 'intangible benefits', but these too will be readily exploited by the perceptive and those with an eye for the commercial impact of process efficiencies.

- Hanson Aggregates found, within a year of implementing electronic invoice receipt from key suppliers, that they had saved time measured to be four person-days per month. This was even more notable given that during the first year they only received about 10% of their invoices electronically. Their total set-up and running costs had been less than £3000, and this had more than been saved within 18 months.

- Kvaerner Construction gained six days additional time to prepare a tender submission on a contract, valued at £25 million, by exchanging electronic bill of quantities data with the quantity surveyor. The information was available to their estimators sooner and with greater confidence in its accuracy.

2.3.3 Where should we look for the benefits?

Some of the people I talk with find it hard not to see electronic exchange as being purely a way to save on stamps. Such a perspective normally precedes their impressing on me how many invoices they can get into one envelope. Certainly postage, and all its incumbent facets, is one area where benefits are found. However, the main opportunities lie in understanding the costs associated with wasteful, often duplicated activities and in identifying how business processes, including those between companies, can be streamlined.

The first tier of benefits can be identified by considering what could be achieved if you could:

- avoid re-keying or scanning of data
- avoid transcription errors
- access data more quickly
- store and retrieve information electronically
- gain more time for planning.

Then there are several further tiers of benefits accessed by exploiting the broader, commercial implications. Improved operational effectiveness should allow your company to win more business and, hopefully, to improve both the value you add to your customer and, given a fair wind, to your margins. A key objective is to demonstrate how your company adds more client value through your application of EIE technology while at the same time knowing that this increased service is not at the expense of higher internal costs.

Consideration must be given to how the very basis of our business operations can be changed, and not just to how the same processes can be achieved faster and cheaper. Our thinking can be restrained by the large number of process factors we have accepted and have ceased to submit to effective questioning. It is our reticence to challenge the accepted norms that prevents us from achieving a real step change in our fortunes.

The commercial objectives are well rehearsed but we often tackle a problem we can readily influence, rather than the one that has the greatest impact. For example. We generally believe that improved customer–supplier relationships will improve service, lower costs and build loyalty. However, the administrative costs of maintaining high numbers of suppliers drives some companies to reduce their supplier base. This is often aimed at reducing administrative costs and negotiating better price and service levels. However, with standardized EIE it becomes possible to sustain a larger number of suppliers without spiralling administrative costs. An open market will help maintain competitive prices and quality products. The approach can change from 'How do I reduce my supplier base to a manageable level?' to 'How do I obtain the best overall supply service to meet my operational goals?'.

The benefits of EIE certainly involve streamlining existing functions. However, the full value will only be found when you throw away preconceptions and rebuild processes based on this new set of tools. At a macro level, this must be undertaken taking a holistic design, construct and operate perspective.

2.4 Tool or technology?

The increasing interest in trivia-based games has caused us to spend our limited free time wondering about critical matters, such as whether a tomato is a fruit and why it is that a pig is the only animal immune to all snake venom. It is nearly always good to know more today than you did yesterday, but not if gaining this knowledge merely distracts you from something far more important. I confess to enjoying the occasional trivia quiz and have even been known to take cards out of the pack where I believe my answer to be better than the one given. However, unless I need to farm pigs on a fruit-only diet in a snake-infested swamp, the answers to such questions will not help increase my business performance.

Whether electronic information exchange is a tool or technology falls into the same category of trivial thinking. The answer is that it does not matter – just as long as we have exploited the potential it offers to us and our industry. Just as we use the telephone with hardly a second thought, so we should 'use' EIE. Both are technologies that provide an appropriate means of communication. The telephone links people together regardless of where they happen to be, while electronic information links computer applications together in the same way.

Having the right tools for the job makes perfect sense to all who have attempted DIY. EIE is the right tool for integrated computer applications. We will gain from using the tool, but not from debating the technology.

2.5 Misconceptions – mist, myths and mistakes

There are always mist, myths and mistakes linked to anything exalted as being 'new', especially if it is perceived that we have to 'change' for it to perform its wonders. Most are simply inertia dressed up to look like reasoned argument. Innovators have to be able to identify and eliminate these factors without insulting the perpetrator who may only be (and often is) passing on an erroneous perception they have been given in equally good faith. The solution to this problem is something akin to a computer virus checker. Because EIE has been around for some time, it is possible to build up a database of known misconceptions. Then, by carefully understanding how they work, it is possible to identify most new invaders just as quickly. Finally, as with a virus checker, you must flag up the misconception the very first time it is spotted, as delay allows it to spread and gain strength through misguided advocacy.

Three golden rules for data exchange are to remember that it is:

- not difficult
- already proven to work
- does not require traditional rules and business controls to be swept away.

Should someone suggest anything that breaks a golden rule, become instantly suspicious! It should be stressed that those who seed misconceptions into the path of progress nearly always do so in all innocence. The deliberate saboteur is, thankfully, rare, but the confidently incorrect are far too common.

2.5.1 The mist

Unless change comes like a storm in the night, we have time to create a little mist to shroud the subject from clear view. This sounds like a deliberate blocking manoeuvre and, to some, it will be exactly that. For others it is a legitimate evaluation technique that seems to achieve the wrong result. We start off being interested in the benefits but a little wary of the exact route to achieving them. This then raises questions which can be answered, but can't be quantified – which to some means the answer is 'no benefits'. As a result we slowly let the good idea fade into the mist of time, possibly acclaiming, on reflection, that is was a good idea whose day had not yet arrived. Then suddenly the mist clears, and everybody seems to be doing it!

Mist, in this context, is self-generated. It often starts out as a valid, perhaps well-intentioned, line of questioning that never reaches a conclusion, but only raises more questions, such as:

- How will this affect or customer services?
- Will our systems cope with the these requirements over the next five years?
- How many of our competitors are going to do this?
- It may save us a lot of money, but is there something better?
- Shouldn't we write a process impact report first?
- Perhaps we should wait to see what others do?

Given that the construction industry acknowledged the benefits of EIE during the mid-1980s, there is no doubt that we wandered off into 'the mist'.

2.5.2 The myths

Assuming that mist alone is not enough to keep progress at bay, there are always a few well circulated myths to fall back on. The difference between mist and myths is that mist is inertia we create all on our own, whereas a myth is imported inertia. Myths are therefore more dangerous, as they come with ready-made status.

I once worked for a man who demanded market price trends in the same way that a schoolboy craves conkers. Being a loyal member of the team I would supply great quantities of information backed up by evidence and analysis. After several months it became apparent that, although the demand never faltered, nothing I sent was ever accepted at face value. Worse still, it was often used as ammunition to berate my marketing skills. Being young I made two fundamental mistakes. First, I assumed that as he was my boss he must know better. Secondly, that he had marked me out for greater things and was testing my resolve. I therefore carried on and came up with cunning ways to prove my figures, but all to no avail. It was only much later that I discovered he would meet one of my competitors in his local pub and happily took his view on price trends to be the unquestionable truth. After all, I only worked for him.

The point here is to note the power of the myth. We rarely have the luxury, as I eventually did, of discovering the source of a myth. Therefore, the purveyor can attach great status to a myth and do so with confidence and sincerity. Allowed to go unchecked, a myth quickly takes on the persona of an established fact. Some of the more general myths that have hampered electronic data exchange developments are:

- our business (and the entire construction sector) is different
- we need standard trading terms to trade electronically

- we missed EDI, but we are planning to catch the Internet
- it will never happen.

Let's take these one by one.

Our business is different

As discussed earlier in this chapter, in any meaningful way, the answer is 'No we are not'. We design things, buy things, make things, organize things and get wrapped up in lots of administration. Just like everyone else.

We need standard terms and conditions to trade electronically

Why? Sending an order or invoice electronically does not absolve a company from commercial responsibility. Standard terms would be very useful, but it is wrong to require them in greater measure for electronic trading. Behind this premise there lies an element of opportunism. As a parent I soon learnt the trick of association. My daughter refuses to finish her vegetables but then lets on that she would like to ride her bike when we have finished the meal. This is my opening to associate these two unrelated factors. The process on which I have embarked could end up with no vegetables being eaten and my having to find something else for her to play as clearly I can't back down and allow her to ride her bike. If it had worked, I would have been delighted – but the cost of failure must be considered.

To suggest opportunism could be a difficult charge to make stick. However, it is the case that initial attempts to introduce electronic data exchange between contractors and suppliers failed in the late 1980s because standard terms were sought as a prerequisite but then could not be agreed. The result was that no progress was made on either front and a considerable amount of residual caution was generated about trying again.

We missed EDI, but we are planning to catch the Internet

This myth is also a mistake and has wound me up the wrong way on a number of occasions! My frustration was even thought to portray an 'anti-Internet' viewpoint which, just to be on the safe side, is definitely not the case. EDI, or even 'traditional EDI' as it is often referred to, is very much a part of the future. However you look at it or whatever acronym is in vogue at the time, the principles of EDI are more applicable in the Internet era.

The myth is to believe that something new has arrived (the Internet) which has replaced what came before (EDI). But, these are two parts of the same subject and will gain from each other's specific abilities. The Internet will enable us to reach out to many more businesses partners. Equally, Internet developments such as extensible markup language (XML) have used the tried and tested protocols of 'traditional' EDI (i.e. the EDIFACT standards) to support system integration.

There I go again! Falling into the world of techno-babble and terminology that has rightly caused many managers to condemn all involved in this subject to 'file 13'. Let me try and put it another way. Just as we use ordinary phones and feature phones, so we will use different data exchange techniques. We must maintain a business-centred view and not let the multitude of information exchange developments cause us to miss real commercial opportunities.

The mistake would be to decide that the emergence of the Internet makes it sensible to ignore tried and tested opportunities while we wait for the new technology to settle down, promising that, when it does, we shall progress to implementation. As if I needed to make the point again – business managers must cut through the smoke and focus on achieving process benefits.

It will never happen

… It has!

2.5.3 The mistakes

Mistakes are normally the most visible and troublesome of the problems flowing from misconceptions. This is because they are usually

---

Box 2.1 Some basic principles

Communication networks (value added network, Internet provider, etc.) You should only need to be connected to one for each type of exchange

Communications software (EDI software, browser, etc.) One product should handle all your electronic document exchange

Exchange standard (e.g. electronic invoice format) Use as few as possible – hopefully one. Make sure the standard has been correctly defined to any appropriate syntax rules. If it is not, then be prepared to write off most of the set-up costs against this specific trading relationship, as there may be little or no opportunity to add other trading partners via this interface

System interface (i.e. import–export file structure) Use this like a 13 amp plug – protect your system from multiple interfaces. Even if you cannot get all your trading partners to adopt a single exchange standard, each should be linked through a common import–export interface

---

linked to an expenditure decision that has been taken. I always get a bit nervous when a company indicates its willingness to adopt electronic exchange 'when their trading partners request them to do so'. My concerns are threefold.

- Firstly because the 'chicken and egg' form of inertia that can be so incredibly self-supporting.
- Secondly, there is the lost opportunity from not grasping the benefits, even if this means being a little proactive and encouraging trading partners to become involved.
- Finally, and most relevant in this section, comes the risk that, if we wait until we are pushed, mistakes are more likely to be made that build unnecessary costs and inflexibility into data exchange systems.

Seldom in life do we pick up the tricks of the trade the first time we try something new. Equally the assumption that the proactive partner understands how electronic exchange can best be achieved can be overgenerous. The collaborative, industry-wide, approach certainly reduces the risk, but the pitfalls can still be expensive and easily made. A list of some of the main things to check for when implementing electronic exchange is given in *Box 2.1*.

When setting up a new exchange link, the interconnecting nature of the major value added networks (VANs) and the global reach of the Internet means that you and your trading partners do not have to be using the same services provider. If you are on network A and your partner is on network B, neither of you has to join the other's network, provided A and B have an operational interconnection.

The same applies for the data exchange software. You should look to build all links through the one product wherever possible. Should your trading partner use a standard not supported by your product, you will have to consider the alternatives. Such a requirement should generally be resisted, especially where the exchange standard proposed is either outdated or of limited use outside the specific trading relationship. Conversely, if the proposed change opens up a new opportunity (e.g. implementing a new global exchange standard) it may be that you need to move in the direction of your trading partner.

With regard to the exchange standard, if there is a problem implementing the version proposed by your trading partner, always check that they cannot adopt your standard before considering the alternatives – even if they are a customer. They are very likely to know the benefits available from establishing a link with you and may be able to use your standard just as effectively, especially if yours is widely supported.

The system interface is critical (see also Chapter 7), but ultimately where electronic exchange delivers real value to your operations. Writing multiple interfaces is expensive and nearly always avoidable. You may, for commercial reasons, have to use more than one exchange standard, but the final link into your software should be through a single gateway. The apparent short-term benefits of establishing a growing number of bespoke links directly into your software are outweighed by the longer-term problems such an approach can cause. Clearly each interface costs time and money to establish, as well as adding to the ongoing maintenance load. However, perhaps a more critical factor is the impact this has when you come to change software. The single interface separates the transmission of data from its application. Therefore, either can be changed without serious cost implications on the other. Careful interface management will allow you to change transfer mechanism (e.g. from VAN to Internet), or to add new trading partners (even using bespoke standards) without changing your software import–export routines.

The business must be able to progress without being limited by electronic exchange applications, or any other applications for that matter. Such problems are harder to accept where such constraints could be avoided through informed management. This subject is discussed further in Chapter 7.

2.6 Searching for the opportunity

2.6.1 Planning to improve

Achieving benefits through the application of technology is just the same as all other forms of innovation. A good idea is identified and applied in a controlled and targeted manner. All too often we either don't spot the opportunities presented by new technology because we are either too familiar with traditional methods, or we don't apply them because we believe they must involve complications (the 'no pain, no gain' theory). In fact, access to data exchange opportunities has greatly improved as computer power and the inclusion of data exchange capabilities have both increased. It is essential to specify the opportunities being sought at the start of any change process. By this I mean an evaluation of how EIE can be applied to enable a step change in process effectiveness. This can only be achieved by combining a knowledge of the business with an understanding of the capabilities of the technology.

I have often been asked, 'Why, given the universally accepted benefits from electronic exchange, is anyone slow to take it up?'. If they want to twist the knife a little more they might add go on to suggest that, 'If the benefits are considerable, have we just not put the point over well enough?'. The answer I give is that 'We all know that a healthy diet and regular exercise are good for us, but we don't all do that either'. Sometimes we need a reason (preferably one we thought of ourselves!) to gain the necessary personal commitment to change our ways, hopefully before we are forced into it.

We all have lots to think about and to fit in to our busy lives. However, we are often highly motivated to try something new when we can personally identify with the change process. By identifying a particular opportunity that can be realized through the application of data exchange (and experience has been that many can be generated), we achieve progress linked to the all-important principle of 'ownership'.

I am reminded of the frustration experienced by a colleague who had developed several software products that supported EIE in the construction sector. In the usual course of events, programming 'bugs' were identified and aesthetic changes requested by the client until the product was deemed to be acceptable. His frustration came whenever he had to upgrade or modify a product that he knew had yet to be used in anger. In contrast, I could present him with problems relating to an 'operational' product and he would seemingly relish the task. Well, almost! The point is, the purpose of the technology he provided was that it was used to save someone time and money and not merely to impress.

Perhaps I am getting old and cynical as, time and again, I am stunned by how straightforward 'leading-edge' practices really are when you get to see them 'in the flesh'. I have never found anything remotely like astrophysics in good business systems, just clear, simple and well-reasoned operating principles. The 'impressive' applications, to my mind, are those that have delivered clear business processes in the most simple and intuitive manner. The trick is not to fall for the technology and the impressive list of features laid out before you.

We need a desire to use technology, but this must remain subordinate to a clear business objective. Therefore, when promoting the adoption of EIE, my preferred approach is always to base actions on clearly identifying business needs. The principle that says, 'progress is more readily achieved by removing obstacles than in pushing harder', is absolutely right. If more 'push' worked best we would all be a lot further forward. The key business opportunities must be revisited and the obstacles to their achievement clearly identified. The next step is to identify those obstacles which the new technology can remove.

Examples of the incorrect application of new technology can be a cause for some amusement, but must be an encouragement to the rest of us to ensure we don't follow the same road. Failure to exploit the full potential of technology can be an expensive business. Construction companies can seldom be said to spend money unwisely, but they can waste a great deal inadvertently by not adopting proven technology. The numerous opportunities available from the effective use of information provide a rich source of innovation fodder. Fortunately for the humanists amongst us, their correct deployment is dependent on the vision and commercial insight of business managers. The technical application is often extremely simple, but the impact can be to deliver a revolutionary process change.

2.6.2 Planned innovation

How then do we discover these treasures? Much progress will come from following our gut instincts, and still more by copying changes adopted by others. Personally, I prefer a more structured approach, but one that draws on both the aforementioned drivers. According to a book I once read on the subject, innovation is 'the attacker's advantage'.[3] Thus we need to be able to go and find our bit of innovation before the battle is lost. I have had a few good ideas in the bath and a couple lying awake in the middle of the night, but I find this approach is a touch haphazard, and it often fails to deliver ideas that stand up to serious scrutiny.

A structured approach to identifying business opportunities, involving operational managers, has never yet failed to provide drivers for innovation. Further still, these ideas are specific to each individual business and are 'owned' by those who will be involved in their delivery. Careful management of the process together with knowledge of enabling technology can open doors previously considered to be barred.

Innovation needs to start from a clear understanding of the business anatomy. From there it is possible to set out to find the changes that can be delivered and which enable progress in a desirable commercial direction. The business anatomy is a reference point which we need to use to test the validity of opportunities and obstacles identified within the process. By anatomy I mean to embrace everything from the mission statement to a view on the company's attitude to risk or capital investment. These premises may themselves need to be challenged, and so at least some involvement from senior executives is fundamental to this approach.

So, this book is about identifying desirable business opportunities that can be delivered using proven technology and to ensure they are implemented effectively.

2.7 Security and legal concerns

2.7.1 General concerns

If we are to gain the full benefits of EIE, security and legal concerns must be resolved. Some concerns are legitimate, but there are many more that result from misinformation or simply a lack of information. The following list sets out some of the concerns that have been raised:

- Will my data arrive safely?
- How can I be sure who sent the message? (Authentication)
- Can the sender authorize the actions contained in the message? (Authorization)
- Is it unfair to send an electronic message when others can still only handle paper?
- Can I use electronic information as evidence in a dispute?

The law does not prescribe specific answers to all these questions. Some people perceive this as a cause for concern, but it is simply the way UK law operates. When something goes to court we may get a ruling that can be used to clarify a particular point. Occasionally there will be Government action, such as that supporting the use of digital signatures and certificates. Most of the time it is down to business partners to agree an acceptable working arrangement for electronic exchange. Given the heated arguments that surround attempts by governments to legislate how we should conduct our affairs it is perhaps better not to seek blanket rules to cover complex and diverse business practices.

Many legal and security concerns raised in connection with electronic business have no basis when compared to traditional methods. In other words, the requirement was not applied to paper-based communications. Into this category fall questions such as:

- How can I be sure my electronic document has arrived?
- Is the transfer route 100% secure?
- How do I know they will process my data correctly?
- Could someone intercept my message?
- Will the receiver recognize this as a valid document?

There is a 'back foot' as well as a 'front foot' answer to such questions.

The 'back foot' answer (take a deep breath) is to point out that traditional document exchange was achieved by stuffing a piece of flammable material inside an envelope, dropping it into a post-box, allowing it to be handled by unknown people and machines through the sorting office (at least once), stuffing it into a sack to be paraded openly up and down the street until it was dropped into an unspecified receptacle at the recipient's premises – no doubt without the inclusion of a reply slip which could then be signed and returned the same way.

The 'front foot' answer is to note the additional security and legal facilities provided by electronic exchange. Such options include:

- data exchange networks providing audit trail and document backup services
- options for auto-acknowledging the receipt of messages (within seconds!)
- data verification checks built into messages
- message encryption options
- digital certificates, to confirm message status.

2.7.2 Interchange agreements

Where absolutely necessary, companies can adopt an interchange agreement to set out the rules governing electronic interchange. These, to my mind, are high value, high hassle, documents that should only be used where absolutely necessary. This view largely comes from knowing that such agreements are rarely, if ever, used for paper-based business transactions. It also stems from having watched companies start out believing that they must use an interchange agreement but ending up operating without even requiring message acknowledgement. One last concern about interchange agreements is that they can quickly put off the majority of small to medium sized companies from adopting electronic exchange. Let's face it, how many of us would even use e-mail if we have to sign a legal document and define an operations manual (part of most interchange agreements) before sending our first message?

2.7.3 Security and confidence – digital signatures and certificates

In 1999 the Government introduced an electronic commerce bill to aid the development of electronic exchange. Some lawyers have implied that the bill is not required to provide a legal status but does put in place the framework for those wishing to issue digital certificates, etc. Either way, this was part of a Europe-wide initiative to increase the percentage of business transacted electronically.

A digital signature (Dsig) normally implies the use of public and private key encryption. This is where the sender encrypts the message using what is known as their 'private key' and the receiver decrypts the message using the 'public key'. By this mechanism the receiver can be sure that the message has been sent by the private key holder.

A digital certificate (Dcert) can also be used to convey a defined level of authorization (e.g. an ordering limit or payment guarantee) to backup the electronic message. These are controlled and provided by 'issuing bodies' who share the responsibility should a problem occur (not caused by misuse). In essence, the digital certificate acts a bit like a cheque guarantee card when making a payment.

Dsig says this message is from a particular person (or company), and Dcert confirms this fact and may also provide the necessary authority required to give the recipient confidence to act on its contents.

There will undoubtedly be many specific uses for certificate in the future, but three key applications have been identified for early use in the construction industry:

- identification certificates (provide details about who sent the message)
- procurement certificates (e.g. to confirm a buyer's authority to purchase)
- one-off certificates (e.g. a payment guarantee).

Certificates could be held on a PC or, for added security, on a smart card with a PIN access code or on an issuer's Web site. Certificates can be applied to an electronic message or a file or used within a networked trading system, as required.

A further construction related application is to provide file integrity when exchanging a 'native' file (i.e. a proprietary software file that could be loaded into another copy of the same software and manipulated), such as a CAD file. This could be protected by applying the certificate to a drawing or by registering a drawing, with its certificate, in an archive. Therefore, even if the recipient altered the drawing, the originally transmitted file could always be verified.

2.7.4 Intellectual property

This is not a concern related just to EIE but one which has been with us since information has had an intrinsic value of its own. Certainly the freedom with which information can now be copied and distributed has raised the profile of this issue. As David Bicknell put it when writing in *Computer Weekly*[4] 'effective intellectual property protection is vital if e-commerce is truly to take off'. The originators of information, users and service providers all have to take appropriate steps to provide the necessary protection. The article went on to quote the Alliance for Electronic Business, who set out a number of key points:

- there should be a focus on regulating behaviour and not just on technology
- users who infringe are liable, not the businesses that provide the products which facilitate infringement
- there must be a reliance on existing and enforceable copyright laws
- a harmonized intellectual property framework should be developed to match the harmonized legal framework
- the degree of liability must be related to the degree of control that each party has in determining the content of a message.

European Union directives on copyright and associated liability, together with the campaign spearheaded by the World Intellectual Property Association (WIPO), were seen by David Bicknell to be essential if we are to effectively update laws and regulations to provide confidence to the owners of information.

The debate about intellectual property rights now has to take the world wide Web into account. For many business transactions this is not really a point of concern. Where there is a genuine concern, such as with design information or copyright, confidence in the protection of intellectual property rights may be they key to unlock further electronic exchange progress. The Government legal framework covering the use of digital signatures and certificates will help in some cases. Ultimately, property holders will need to seek redress through national and international law (WIPO comes under the United Nations) where their rights are infringed.

2.7.5 Electronic evidence

Concern has often been expressed as to the validity of electronic documents during legal claims between companies. Thankfully there have now been a number of cases where electronic documents have been challenged in court and the ruling has been to confirm that such electronic documents are admissible as evidence. The Civil Evidence Act 1995 introduced a system wherby all documents and copy documents, including computer records, can be admitted as evidence in civil procedings. As with paper documents, the management system controlling the flow of information within a company is important. Electronic documents need to be received, archived and processed correctly.

2.7.6 Unfair practice

The best example of unfair practice is that of electronic tendering. A number of quantity surveyors and consultants indicated they could not send out electronic documents as some of the bidding contractors were not set up to utilize the electronic option. This gives an unfair advantage to those able to utilize the electronic file. As well as being a recipe for stagnation, this is also an incorrect assumption. It would only be unfair if the contractors were not all given the same opportunity. Were some contractors refused the electronic file while others were given it, then this would indeed constitute unfair practice. It may be necessary in some cases to provide a paper and electronic option, but it is not necessary to force all to work according to the lowest common denominator. Those with experience of EIE, such as retail companies, expect suppliers to exchange electronic documents. It is already being muted by some construction industry client bodies that tender prequalification may require an ability to support electronic exchange.

3

Rising to meet the challenge

Construction companies can seldom be accused of spending money unwisely, but they can waste a great deal inadvertently. Through collaboration, even the inadvertent waste is now being tracked down.

3.1 Trust us to collaborate

When inventing anything to do with open communication it seems a good idea to at least consider adopting a universal approach.

We may be tempted to make disingenuous comments about the construction industry, but during the mid- to late 1990s a decision of great vision, not to mention fundamental importance, was taken. The major contractors, suppliers and professional services agreed to work together to establish a common basis for the development and implementation of electronic information exchange (EIE). It was also agreed to adopt, wherever possible, standards that were based on international formats.

In a report entitled *The Future of the Construction Industry – Leading the Change*, produced by the Henley Centre,[5] the impact of collaboration was looked at and the findings summarized as follows:

> By collaborating, companies in the industry can determine how technology will deliver the services they require from it. There are likely to be considerable benefits in sharing ideas on how technology might transform working practices and raise productivity.

The report went on to say:

> Our analysis suggests that the conditions are ripe for construction companies to collaborate with clients, providers of other services and each other to raise the performance of the industry and thus create benefits for both themselves and their clients.

Where collaboration is not present, two barriers arise which reduce the commercial benefits from electronic communications. First, there will be multiple data exchange formats, or languages, simply because the chances of commonality are as remote as the infamous monkey typing Shakespeare. Secondly, multiple localized and overlapping implementation initiatives will come into play as each group promotes the adoption of its solution in an understandable attempt to keep down their set-up costs.

The law of the jungle could then be allowed to sort out the ensuing mess. The simple truth is that this sort of battle would, at the very least, set back open information exchange by many years. At worst, it could prevent not only the adoption of a universal solution but also the widespread adoption by the majority of companies. A large number of business managers would watch from the sidelines, commending themselves on deciding to do nothing. There would be no clear alternative option for us to lay before them as we had justified inertia by the very complexity of the attempted solution. Meanwhile, the industry bleeds inefficiently as waste continues to hamper innovation and fragmentation prevents process re-engineering.

3.1.1 Multiple languages

The early pioneers in the field of electronic trading can be excused for not waiting for an international standard to emerge. However, by developing a range of national and sectoral standards to facilitate early progress, the longer term objective of open communication was seriously hampered. Just as with spoken languages, a cultural identity soon develops alongside a desire to avoid change – unless, that is, everyone else agrees to change to use your language. The 'early adopters' were able to make progress, but for a reason such as this, a universal move to trade electronically did not quickly follow.

3.1.2 Early initiatives

Many major corporations 'rolled out' electronic exchange to their trading partners. This was generally an effective way to make progress but was prone to propagate many different, albeit often only slightly, approaches. Termed 'hub and spokes' roll out, it openly confirms the priority it gives to the company at the 'hub'. It is also an eloquent descriptor for painful experiences by any company that ends up on the end of many different 'spokes' in an attempt to support good customer relations.

The construction sector cannot be said to have been inactive in trying to roll out electronic exchange during the early electronic data interchange (EDI) period (post-Jurassic). Clients, contractors and suppliers had identified the benefits available from electronic exchange and sought to capitalize upon them. During the late 1980s and early 1990s, I was working for one of the major suppliers of steel reinforcement in the UK construction sector. Approaches were made by contractors looking to implement electronic exchange. Two main factors appeared to mitigate against progress. First, though not to my mind proven conclusively, suppliers were concerned there was no unified approach to ensure they would not end up on the end of several different spokes. Secondly, and clearly the damning factor in our particular case, was an attempt by some contractors to require standard terms and conditions of trading to be agreed as a prerequisite to implementing electronic exchange. Agreeing standards terms and conditions of trading may be a laudable objective but, as this objective was not achieved, neither was electronic trading.

The early progress that was made came on the retail wing of the construction industry. In particular builder's merchants and suppliers who traded with DIY outlets were encouraged to implement electronics exchange. These often followed the hub and spokes approach and adopted the UK's Tradacoms exchange standard, but did provide a core of companies that had not only identified the benefits, but had experienced them as well. Their enthusiasm for further progress clearly helped when, during the mid-1990s, a collaborative attempt was made finally to make electronic exchange happen in the construction industry.

3.1.3 EDICON (EDI (Construction) Ltd) – the early construction industry initiative

As I write this section, I am preparing to head into London on the early train tomorrow morning for the last EDICON AGM. At this meeting this initiative will formally be wound up and its spirit will be joined with that of the CITE initiative to take forward the EIE mantle. I have even dug out my EDICON tie to wear for the occasion. The fact that I have had this tie for over 10 years says much more about the construction industry than it does about EDICON.

The following details are based on an article written about EDICON in one of its newsletters,[6] and outlines how EDICON was formed and how it provided a central voice for the industry before finally combining forces with the Construction Industry Trading Electronically (CITE) initiative. While most of the industry remained unaffected by the emergence of international data exchange developments, EDICON gave us a voice at the table. It also provided a forum under which we could consider the implications and practicalities of exchanging information other than on pieces of paper. Eventually the need to drive forward implementation activities led to the formation of CITE, and the rest, so they say, is history.

In 1987, EDICON was formed as an association of companies that had realized that EDI would play a major part in the way business was transacted in the years ahead. Clearly, standards were required and it was important that the UK construction industry had a say in the way this was achieved. Through the substantial voluntary efforts of the companies involved, EDICON became established at the UN/ EDIFACT Board as a major contributor to development activities. Later on, EDICON was instrumental in the formation of a pan-European implementation group, known as EDIBUILD. Thus, EDICON has continued to play its part in the cooperative and collaborative process of using information exchange technology to help improve the building process.

In the late 1980s, EDICON developed its own implementation groups but, with the recession, companies cut the effort being put into such projects and maintained 'watching briefs'. This, understandably, depleted much of the essential impetus required to achieve the objective of operational services. As the recession levelled out, a number of companies, led by the major contractors, looked again at how to implement EIE solutions with their trading partners. It was recognized that a pragmatic approach would be needed and that a facilitator was important. Interlock (an independent company formed from within the industry, specifically to support EIE initiatives) became the facilitator and an initiative was launched with the express objective of implementing EIE solutions for its members. The CITE initiative was born.

Despite concerns in some quarters, there was no duplication of effort between EDICON and CITE, as the two were complementary. Many companies and individuals were involved in both. While EDICON maintained the broad remit and international links, CITE concentrated on 'making it happen'. Recognizing that liaison begins at home, EDICON established links with the UK EIE association. This association has changed names twice in the last few years, first from the EDI Association (EDIA) to become the Electronic

Commerce Association (ECA) and now, following a merger with the Article Number Association (ANA) it has become eCentre^{UK}. Clearly the battle of names I eluded to earlier has not been restricted to the construction industry. This association allowed EDICON members to get involved in cross-industry issues, such as financial EDI (or FEDI) – a subject covered in Chapter 8 of this book.

Following the creation of CITE, it was always envisaged that EDICON would concentrate on the strategic issues both in support of its members and also as a voice in outside organizations and bodies. Through meetings and special interest groups, EDICON sought to satisfy the wide-ranging interests of member companies within the EIE arena. The involvement of the members' companies remained important, as was the need to retain a focus on EIE as being a business issue, not a technical one.

The combined CITE and EDICON organization must provide a coordinated and effective approach to EIE, advice and development within the Construction Industry. The industry must exploit it. So, as I pack up my last set of AGM papers, I will remind myself that I too was one of the business managers who failed to exploit EIE when the subject was first raised by EDICON. A bit of nostalgia, perhaps. A sense of urgency to deliver the objective, certainly. Concern that we could still fail to appreciate the merit of a collaborative approach, absolutely!

3.2 Creating simplicity

> Simplicity is the user's dream but the inventor's loss of income.

To make progress with electronic exchange, it soon became abundantly clear that it had to be made simple to achieve. It also needed to be simple to understand in commercial terms, as the decision to adopt such a change needed to be taken by senior managers. So, how do you make something that entails such technical complexity simple to achieve, within an industry known to suffer the occasional attack of nerves and inertia?

Three ways to impress are:

- Make even the most complicated task look so simple that everyone thinks it's easy enough to have a go, at which point they discover just how clever you are.
- Make a really simple task look so complicated that no one dares to have a go and happily pays you to do it for them.
- Make each job look just as difficult as it really is so that, when anyone decides to try it for themselves they find out what an honourable and knowledgeable person you are ... and instantly wants to appoint you to a senior position and asks you how to erect flat-pack furniture.

Those who enjoy making things sound difficult, either habitually or professionally, are always on the look out for new opportunities. I suppose writing a letter could be made to sound hideously difficult. By breaking it down into its constituent parts and highlighting the required skills of dexterity, character sequencing and the patience it requires, many people could quickly be put off the idea. The truth is we would not get away with such a hypothesis, as it is well known that writing is a skill that can be mastered at an early age, given good health and education, and practised throughout our lifetime with little thought.

Then along comes EIE – an ideal opportunity for 'complexity promoters'! The list of hurdles quickly builds up. For example:

- There are lots of different software packages, so we need lots of bespoke solutions.
- With operating platforms from PCs to mainframes, there is clear incompatibility.
- Who would ever trust an electronic document?
- This will require competing software providers to cooperate.
- Data transfer involves a multitude of mind boggling technical protocols.

These, and many more, are genuine concerns. However, despite what many may try to tell you, these concerns do not need to stand in the way of simplicity. Indeed, not only are there theoretical 'simple' solutions, but the construction industry has shown the vision to grasp them. Every day of our lives we use many highly complex contraptions without a second thought. We open car doors by squeezing a piece of plastic and yet, apart from the enlightened few, we have no idea what is inside let alone which standard was employed to ensure nextdoor's car didn't open at the same time! The principle we adopt is a simple one. It works, it is beneficial, therefore we use it. This is one of the key principles behind 'creating simplicity'.

There are answers to the points noted above, which I shall now touch on briefly. At the same time, it is worth considering why we are asking these questions. Is it to help improve business performance through a more effective implementation, or are we sometimes looking to see if we can find enough complexity to justify a wait and see decision?

Taking each of the above points in turn:

- Each software package could interface with one common exchange language.
- Exchange standards can be formatted in a way that can be openly supported.
- Industry, commerce, the Inland Revenue, Government and many more besides.
- Software companies have supported open exchange – it actually helps them. I am not aware of anyone that decides to purchase a new system because it can't be interfaced!

During the mid-1990s, major contractors, suppliers and professional services companies recognized the need for a common and pragmatic approach to information exchange. For various reasons, overcomplex approaches to open communication had failed – now we needed to go back to basics.

If you want to be able to talk to friends in far away places, you buy a phone line and a phone and start to use it. You don't have to learn about telecommunications theory or network protocols, and you don't ask each friend if they have a compatible phone. If you want to trade electronically you should take the same approach. You want an interface to the outside world and a communications network connection (which could even be your phone and a modem). It is true to say that, until everyone catches on to the idea, you will need to check that each trading partner has a compatible system.

Starting to exchange electronic data clearly requires technical expertise on someone's part. Considerable skill is involved and your data zips around the globe across fibre optic networks at mind-numbing speeds. I am not devaluing these skills, rather I am pointing out that they are available to be exploited. The simplicity that has been created is founded on the collaboration that has delivered common standards and operational support services. These allow business managers to grasp the benefits provided by integrated processes at greatly reduced cost and dramatically increased benefits. A bespoke service between two companies is expensive and, by its very nature, limited in scope. A common exchange format drives down set-up costs and is potentially limitless in scope.

3.3 Better late than early

We did not win the race, but we capitalized on an appalling start!

Much as I hate to admit it, the construction industry has gained from being late into the world of electronic data exchange. To suggest that this was a considered policy would be sophistry, and to continue to delay implementation any further would be sheer madness.

There are some organizations which make it quite clear that they will never be the first to implement anything. With the exception of Adam and the apple, there are few other times when this approach should ever be adopted rigidly. However, we must not allow the success that flowed from ducking the issue to promote this approach to ongoing data exchange developments.

Kings and queens of old were well advised to wait to see what happened to their food taster before sampling the banquet. But, once the feast was declared safe, further abstinence was unnecessary. The implementation of EIE is dependent on at least two people participating. Ultimate success demands majority support, and this is one instance where the wait and see approach can neither be recommended, nor defended. Deciding never to be first is a policy that should be exposed to a good psychologist:

- Was it a bad experience during childhood or perhaps the consequence of being taught good manners?
- Was it the failure of previous expenditure plans or did your first boss tell you how your predecessor lost their job?
- Is it part of the herding instinct or just a lack of time to reach a decision to move?
- Perhaps it is simply a twitch from the sceptic nerve or a mistrust of anyone trying to sell you anything at all.

3.4 Why get close, when effective will do?

> Business partnering is about good business, not about good friends ... though that is always a bonus!

There has probably never been a time when business managers were not considering how to work more effectively with their trading partners. Historically, such relationships have moved forward through improved mutual respect and a recognition that one needs the other to achieve their respective commercial objectives. Historical partnerships that were primarily based on self-interest probably did less damage than would be the case today. This would have been due to fragmentation and more clearly defined responsibilities resulting in a trading partnership that was predominantly administrative. Today, effective project management demands that all involved focus on a common objective. Partnering benefits can be simple or significant, but no business should operate without regard for the overall impact of their actions or inactions. The drive for internal efficiency will continue, but richer seams run within the ambit of overall process effectiveness.

Delivering sufficient value to remain competitive has required companies to work out how to improve the achievement of the overall objective. Individual contributions delivered in a manner that unlocks benefits elsewhere are required. Perhaps more importantly, so is the vision to spot how such value can be delivered. Today's business partnerships are moving from respect to reliance – a trend which is likely to continue.

What has this got to do with electronic information? In order to deliver overall project benefits, first you need to combine the fragmented elements into a single process. If manual data exchange continues to be the way partners link their systems together, the fragments will remain clearly defined and a constraint to re-engineering efforts. This is not to say that we should move to large integrated companies. In fact, the opposite may well deliver the greatest benefit. Specialist subcontractors and suppliers are increasingly being used to maximize the level of expertise across the complex range of activities required by a construction project. This creates more potential for fragmentation, and so could run counter to the drive for a streamlined process.

What we need, is the ability to combine any number of specialists within an integrated process. What is more, this will have to be achieved without great expense, time delays or interference with established working practices. For this to be possible, the people and their computer systems must be able to work together. Which brings me to electronic information. The human interface is by no means a foregone conclusion, but we are inherently flexible, accommodating and determined to make the job work (well, most of us!). In comparison, computers are inherently set in their ways, intolerant and completely oblivious to the task in question.

The option to deliver partnering by removing computers from the equation will bring cheer to all that have suffered at the hands of application errors. However, the construction industry is increasingly reliant on computer software, a trend that is unlikely to change in the foreseeable future. Thus, if we are to achieve effective trading part-nerships, first we need to make sure that our computer applications understand the critical role they are required to play. Our computers need to be taught how to speak nicely to all their other computer friends and not to get moody and uncooperative when we tell them to break off one relationship and to make a new connection with some-one else. An ability to each speak the other person's language is as beneficial for computers as it is for international businessmen. When the boss is jumping up and down (metaphorically, of course!) demanding work commences without delay, it would not be helpful to confess that you have not been able to understand a word the client has said. Our applications must readily interface with each other.

Over recent years, we have become used to being able to do ever more exciting things with our own software. Sadly, many people and business cultures need a greater appreciation of the accessibility and benefits of the exchange of electronic exchanging information with others. Computers help us to perform our jobs more effectively, but we must stop reverting to paper and the phone to interact with our trading partners.

The time has come when we need to teach our software a new lan-guage. This language has to be independent of the operating system or package we use and be common for the sending and receiving system. Once this is achieved, we can piece together a fully integrated project team comprising the skilled individuals and their operating systems. Whether we like our trading partners or not, we must be able to exchange electronic information with them, in an effective way. Only then will we truly be able to deliver integrated projects with any confidence.

4

How did they do that?

Considerable confidence can flow from one dove failing to return to its old resting place.

Just as cat owners take comfort from knowing that 8 out of 10 of their peers recommend a certain brand of canned 'whatever it is', so managers like to know that others have tried tested and recommended new technology. We rightly try to learn how other companies have implemented electronic exchange and seek to benefit from an understanding of their good and bad experiences. That they have done anything at all is often a primary motivating factor. The hours spent preparing a detailed business plan are meat a drink to the committed and the pioneering. The evidence of my own experience is that such documents seem far less potent than the simple disclosure that 'someone else has done this'.

For years the benefits of electronic information exchange (EIE) were preached from the seminar rostrum to the massed ranks of the 'theoretically' converted. Knowing that no one had actually done anything provided a sense of comfort, even justification, to a mutual state of inactivity. Today, this comfort zone has been destroyed with more and more companies becoming 'practically' converted.

The practical experience of the pioneers certainly helps encourage others to adopt new ways of working. Those that have adopted electronic exchange have confirmed the benefits as well as their desire to increase the number of like-minded trading partners they have. How did they cross the Rubicon, and what happened to them on they way?

4.1 Practical examples – non-construction industries

Electronic commerce has energized businesses across a diverse range of industries. The construction sector has much to gain from their experiences, if only from increased confidence. The following examples give a small glimpse at the mounting evidence, much taken from previously published case studies, that EIE has been well proven as a deliverer of commercial benefits.

4.1.1 H & R Johnson Tiles

Faced with increased competition, particularly from imports, coupled with ever rising customer expectation, H & R Johnson Tiles adopted electronic data interchange (EDI) in the early 1990s.[7] Since then, the UK's leading ceramic tile manufacturer has benefited from shortened lead times, improvements in customer service, and reductions in errors and administration costs.

In less than four years EDI has enabled the Stoke-on-Trent, Staffordshire-based company to triple the number of all transactions, with 20% fewer staff using phones and typing orders into the system. Now more than three-quarters of its order transactions are delivered electronically. EDI has also meant that the company can receive and fulfil orders also within a week.

4.1.2 SEI Macro Group

For the SEI Macro Group, which distributes electronic components to industry, the use of EDI its key to improving customer service.[8] With more than 10 years' experience of electronic commerce, the group believes EDI provides a competitive edge by reducing time to market, enhancing quality and reducing costs in the supply chain which spans component maker, distributor and equipment manufacturers. The group, which represents more than 38 of the world's leading electronic and PC components manufacturers, uses the Electronic Data Interchange for Administration, Commerce and Transport (EDIFACT) messaging standard to integrate EDI with its main sales and purchase in computer systems.

4.1.3 Reckitt & Colman – EDI development

Reckitt & Colman plc is an international manufacturer of household and pharmaceutical products employing approximately 17 000 people around the world. Established in 1840, the company manufactures in more than 30 countries, sells products in more than 170 countries and has annual revenues of approximately US $4 billion. Reckitt & Colman Europe is the second biggest company within the Reckitt & Colman group, after the US division, and they started using EDI within their French operations during 1993 and massively integrated EDI in 1995.[9] They totally reorganized their logistics to improve the quality of their service. The EDI set-up was aimed at optimizing the flow of goods and information between the various parts of the logistic chain, and also to reduce the delivery time and administrative work.

Two categories of electronic exchange were developed, one with distributors and one with logistic partners. Reckitt & Colman started EDI with the retailers (product catalogue), and up to 70% of their turnover with them is now done via EDI. Besides this, 100% of wholesalers' orders for non-prescription drugs are transmitted electronically. In order to optimize the physical flow, in May 1995 they developed the sending and reception of EDI messages for transport orders and delivery information. It enables them to know when their mission was executed and gives a status to each of the consignments (delivered/not delivered). This information, directly integrated in the system of client management at Reckitt & Colman, enables them to follow the service quality of forwarders and to inform clients about any problems.

The experience and trust acquired since 1993 has enabled Reckitt & Colman to enter a more mature phase in the development of EDI and to set up more elaborate applications and projects, such as invoicing, advice of shipment and shared management of stocks. The last phase is to integrate a system of stock management that calculates for each warehouse the average of the goods in and goods out, and builds up statistics. This will give the warehouses and trading partners the necessary information (requirements in terms of stock in each warehouse) to prepare the appropriate order.

Convinced by the good results of the French EDI implication, Reckitt & Colman's European

management asked the French logistic team to duplicate their work throughout Europe.

4.1.4 EDI makes the headlines[10]

The newsagents are bulging with titles covering every topic, from knitting to mountaineering, and keeping the news flowing onto the shelves was seen to be an ideal job for EDI. Major developments in the introduction of EDI, using the UK EDIFACT sales report messages, have improved supply chain management and customer service levels in the newspaper and magazine sales industry.

One such initiative was spearheaded by Johnsons News, a major UK independent news wholesaler, which ran a special project focused on setting up EDI links with its retail customers to monitor sales. This enabled Johnsons to provide the first comprehensive sales-based replenishment (SBR) system in the news industry, leading to increased sales through greater availability of products, and improving the ordering function for both wholesaler and retailer.

The Bath-based company, which handles more than 3500 mainstream titles, implemented UK EDIFACT messages – using the GE Information Services Tradanet network – with two of its biggest customers, store chain W. H. Smith and supermarket giants Safeways Stores. On a broader front, it has made its SBR available to many of its independent customers, setting up EDI links with a multitude of different electronic point-of-sale (EPOS) systems, to bring them the benefits of electronic trading.

Retail Technology Manager Andy Watkins said:

> In setting up EDI links with our customers we are learning much more about selling patterns in store and for the first time we're able to monitor stock levels.
>
> EDI has also enhanced our supply management and associated systems and we're able to review and react to the current issue in sale. The use of EDI in the supply chain is a good example of how technology can be used to drive the business and close the information gaps that currently exist.

Jock Ockwell, EDI project manager at W. H. Smith Retail, said initiatives such as the provision of EPOS data via EDI and the supply process using the Johnsons' SBR system had helped improve product availability. He pointed out:

> The cost of waste in the news industry is very large and labour intensive. With SBR, the levels of waste in the supply chain between WH Smith and its wholesalers, such as Johnsons News, is capable or substantial reduction since stock replenishment is based on the most recent actual sales rather than intuitive ones.

Using a new form of EDI, a supply management project carried out by Safeway Stores has resulted in a 9% increase in product availability, a 2% boost in sales and a 7% improvement in efficiency. Advances championed by Johnsons News followed a conference the company convened to encourage the news trade to agree a standard approach to EDI. The UK EDIFACT sales report message was unanimously welcomed by delegates.

4.2 Practical examples – construction related

4.2.1 Tendering case study[11a]

Overview

This case study will be of interest to clients, quantity surveyors and contractors who would benefit from a reduction in manual data processing during the tendering process. Using a number of practical examples, it shows how electronic tender documents, especially bills of quantities, can be exchanged between bill production and estimating software using a standardized electronic format. Contractors, clients, quantity surveyors and software providers have collaborated to provide a common transfer format. As a result, data are now being exchanged between organizations using a range of different commercial and bespoke software systems.

Summary

The construction industry is no stranger to the transfer of large documents (i.e. often running to hundreds of pages) and the burden this places on professionals and profitability alike. This is perhaps most evident during the tendering process when multiple sets of bulky documentation are processed by several bidding contractors, subcontractors and quantity surveyors. The tendering process provides the information upon which all subsequent project activities are founded. Therefore accuracy and efficiency are of considerable importance.

To eliminate waste and non-value-added activities from the construction process, effective project integration is essential. To achieve this, information exchange between computer systems must be cost-

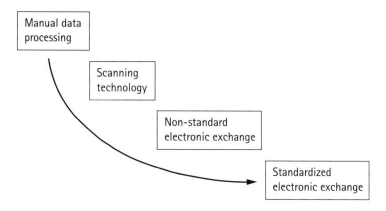

Figure 4.1 Progress towards standardized tendering information exchange

effective. Therefore, common exchange standards need to be available, accepted and adopted by the industry. This case study shows how the industry has combined forces to implement an operational format that has enabled significant savings to be made during the tendering process.

The process

Given the large quantity of information that is exchanged, and manually processed, during the traditional tender, effective information exchange has always been a critical issue. As technology has allowed, the manual input to the process has been reduced. However, the last step in adopting a standardized exchange format has been primarily a cultural one (*Figure 4.1*).

Traditional tendering requires information created by the client's quantity surveyor to be forwarded to several contractors, who each in turn forward extracts to specialist subcontractors. This requires the same information to be handled many times over as it passes along the chain ... and then it comes all the way back up the line, with prices added (*Figure 4.2*).

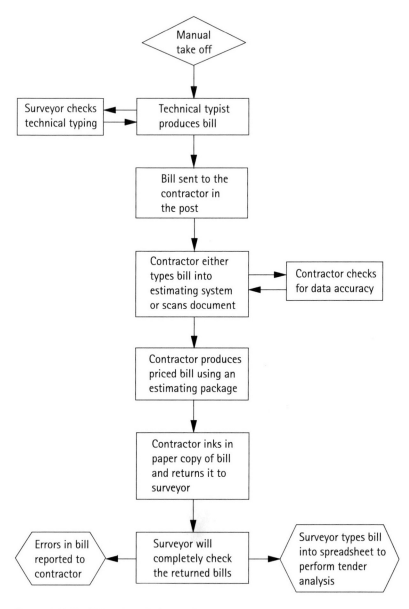

Figure 4.2 Traditional tendering cycle

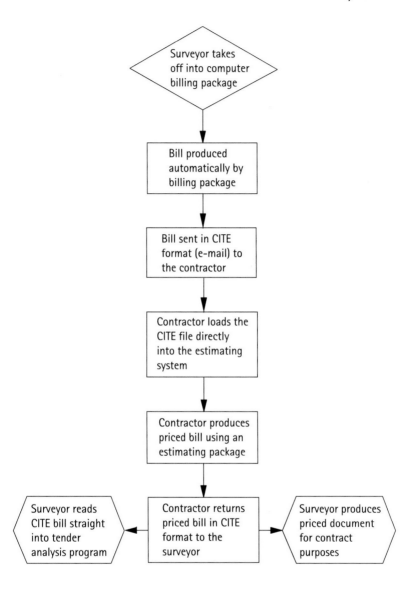

Figure 4.3 Electronic tendering cycle

The use of a standard electronic exchange format has enabled all parties involved in the tendering process to link their systems together. Using a standardized electronic format:

- bill production systems can output tender data
- estimating systems import the tender data
- the contractor can extract and forward work packages for subcontractors
- subcontractors can return prices against these packages
- contractors can submit their tender
- quantity surveyors can import data for bid analysis.

The process becomes a seamless information flow (*Figure 4.3*). Electronic exchange also prevents the high cost and time delays associated with the traditional scanning, re-keying and manual information handling. The process is further transformed by the avoidance of problems or disputes resulting from transcription errors, and further still by linking tender data into valuation and procurement systems.

The approach

Case 1: C. E. Ball. The Cambridge Parkside Leisure Pools project took advantage of the electronic exchange of bill of quantities information when the invitation to tender documents were sent to six contractors. These documents had been prepared by C. E. Ball using their own software. As one of the founding members of the Construction Industry Trading Electronically (CITE), they had previously enabled their software to export bills in the CITE electronic format. Valued at £10 million, the paper documents ran to 472 pages with the electronic equivalent fitting onto a single floppy disk. This electronic version could be read-in by the estimator in under five minutes, enabling the contractor quickly to start preparing their tender submission.

Case 2: DoE Water Service and Charles Brand. During 1997 the Construction Employers Federation supported the introduction of

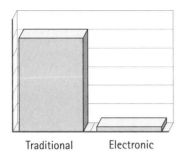

Process savings (per tender issued)
using the CITE electronic exchange:

Basis
• Average bill size 150 pages

Material cost saving
• Paper and copying   £110

Staff time cost saving
• Pre-tender   £90
• Post-tender   £220

Total cost saving   90%

Traditional   Electronic

Figure 4.4 Electronic tender preparation – a client's view. (Source: DoE Water, Northern Ireland)

CITE-based electronic tendering into the Northern Ireland construction industry. Within four months of the project launch the DoE Water Service was able to send a current contract enquiry to the Northern Ireland contractor, Charles Brand.

The project was a £0.5 million reinforced concrete underground service reservoir to be constructed in County Down. The paper documents ran to over 50 pages with the electronic equivalent fitting onto a single floppy disk (220 kilobytes). Although not a large contract by some calculations, the paper version would still take over three hours to scan, format (i.e. define the fields), print and verify before being available within the contractor's estimating system. The electronic version was read-in directly within three minutes – a saving of over 95%.

The DoE Water Service, the client for this project, used their bill production software (Qumic) to create and export the tender in CITE format. This allows the tender documents to be returned electronically, increasing the speed, confidence and effectiveness of tender analysis. On this specific contract amendments to the contractor's systems prevented the priced file being returned within the

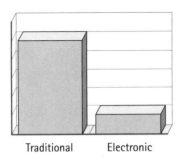

Time reduced by
over 85%

Traditional   Electronic

Figure 4.5 Data entry time comparison. (Source: Kvaerner Construction/The MDA Group UK)

required timescale, although this was subsequently achieved to con-firm that a working interface had been established. Charles Brand used their estimating package (Manifest), which had been upgraded to support them in preparing CITE-based tender submissions. Like many other CITE members, they benefited from the growing number of software providers that support CITE exchange as a feature of their product.

Subsequent analysis carried out by the DoE Water Service (*Figure 4.4*) has highlighted just some of the potential benefits from elec-tronic tendering from the client's perspective. The annual cost of producing, copying and distributing tender documents could be cut by over 90% by adopting electronic exchange. However, these are only the most tangible benefits, which could be dwarfed by those asso-ciated with the impact of time saving throughout the tendering process, the avoidance of transcription errors and the increased speed of bid analysis.

Case 3: Kvaerner Construction and The MDA Group UK. This was a £25 million design and build contract which generated over 3500 measured items for pricing. In paper format this represented 750 pages of information to be processed. Traditionally this would have been scanned, manually checked and then imported into the contractor's (Kvaerner) estimating system. The measured items were provided to Kvaerner by a quantity surveying practice (The MDA Group) working for the contractor. Importing this data took a matter of minutes, and by the end of day 1 the estimator had structured all information ready to commence detailed pricing. For a contract of this size, this represented a saving estimated to be six days.

As more contracts are tendered electronically, the benefits to the estimating process are becoming equally clear. Whether it is a small or multi-million pound contract, the same benefits have been experienced. Tender information is available to the estimator far earlier, and the full descriptions, so often discarded during the scanning phase, can be imported as well. Time savings will vary depending on the size of each tender, but these have been found to be in excess of 80% following analysis provided by Kvaerner (*Figure 4.5*).

As with the client side, this is just the start of a sequence of related benefits. And these benefits flow beyond the estimating process as, on successful tenders, this information may form the basis of the valuation process and procurement activities.

The benefits

Speed. The re-keying or scanning of printed tender information is obviously slower than reading-in an electronic file. Paper bill documents can take hours, sometimes days, to scan, format, check and enter into an estimating system. CITE electronic bill files can be entered directly, normally in under five minutes. This allows more time for tender preparation and can reduce the administrative and overall project costs. The client or quantity surveyor can reduce tender production and distribution costs by over 90%, and estimators can reduce data entry time by over 80%. The bid analysis can be provided more quickly and the tender period could ultimately be reduced.

Accuracy. If a contractor scans a printed tender as input to his estimating system, accuracy has always required a further checking

Field number	1	2	3	4
Field name	Information identifier	Reference	Text	Quantity
Position	0	2–11	13–62	64–74
Field size	1	10	50	11
Field format	an1	an ... 10	an ... 50	n11

Figure 4.6 Part of the CITE electronic tendering standard

process. With CITE bill of quantities messages the accuracy can be 100%.

Process gains. In addition to the obvious gains related to reduced administrative efforts, the client and contractor provide the foundations for further improvements to the procurement, valuation and management processes. There will also be gains available from a faster tender turn around and a faster, more detailed bid analysis available to the client.

Management issues

General. There are two principal barriers to electronic tendering. One is that the electronic tenders are seen by some quantity surveyors to be of greater use to contractors than to themselves, and secondly that the majority of quantity surveying practices have yet to adopt electronic options. This has to be overcome by highlighting the benefits available to the quantity surveyor and their clients. An increasing number of contractors can now handle CITE files, and they are being encouraged to return an electronic version with their bid, even where they initially received only a paper copy.

Unfair practice. Concerns have sometimes been expressed that sending out CITE tenders, when not all contractors could take advantage of them, could be seen as being unfair practice. This is not the case, provided all contractors are afforded the option to receive the electronic version. The use of electronic tenders has been established in the industry for some time. CITE has only promoted the use of a common format, thus improving universal access; and so, if anything, this has increased fairness.

Personnel.   Initial concerns were expressed as to the impact of electronic tendering on the employment prospects for quantity surveyors and estimators alike. In reality electronic exchange allows skilled staff to use more of their skills and spend less time on clerical activities. It is seen as a way to empower the individual, return greater value to their employer and improve service to customers.

Technical aspects.   Data security is often a concern, but it is normally the case that electronic exchange is more secure than traditional paper exchange. The file provides check digits to verify the data integrity and encryption options can be used where this is felt to be appropriate. As with all change, only practical experience will ever address the concerns that are raised.

Viruses are not currently seen as a major concern with electronic data as the exchange format is straight text and not an executable program. However, if program files are included with the transfer to assist the recipient in accessing the data, or executable files (e.g. self-extracting Zip files) are included, then viruses could be present and care must be taken. In all cases the recommended practice is to use an up to date virus-checking system and to check with trading partners that they do likewise.

Software implementation.   The CITE standard developed over the period 1995–1999, though it is now intended to avoid further change for the foreseeable future. Users should always check that their system is compliant with the latest version.

CITE exchange standards.   CITE is providing an increasing range of industry standards. From tenders and valuations to trading documents and project information exchange (i.e. instructions, queries and notices) there are now over a dozen CITE standards available to the industry. Many standards are based on international data standards, though the bill of quantities (BoQ) format was developed on a simple column format to make it easier for software to interface with the standard (*Figure 4.6*).

The CITE BoQ standard sets out the technical structure for the data exchange process alongside operational rules to support those using it operationally. The measured items (BoQ) can be accompanied by an electronic file containing preliminary information. The standard also provides the ability to cross-reference to drawing files, or text notes, which can also be sent in electronic format.

4.2.2 EIE case study[11b]

Overview

This case study will be of interest to contractors, suppliers and manufacturers who would benefit from a reduction in manual data processing and closer partnering during the procurement process. It shows how electronic invoices are being exchanged between companies using a standardized electronic format. Contractors, suppliers and manufacturers have collaborated to provide a common transfer format together with implementation services.

Summary

Hanson Aggregates (formerly ARC), introduced electronic invoicing with their cement suppliers during 1997. The invoice exchange used was that developed under the CITE initiative. The invoices received electronically were integrated directly into the accounts software, cutting out the manual invoice registration operations. As a result of this development, information was also available earlier than previously and without the risk of transcription errors.

The process was initially implemented in the central region and was then replicated in the southern region. Having initially established a link with one supplier, two further links were soon established. Currently, the two regional offices process over 2500 electronic invoices each month. Although one of the pioneers, Hanson experienced few technical problems installing the required technology. Once operational, the electronic invoicing system has basically run itself.

The benefits, analysed by Hanson Aggregates South, have demonstrated some clear tangible benefits, particularly savings on time spent on manually registering invoices. Further benefits came from the commercial value of closer links with key suppliers and from the confidence in data accuracy and fast availability. The challenge now is to increase the number of trading partners and to extend the scope of their electronic trading activities to include orders and other messages.

(Note: Reference here is to Hanson Aggregates, though for much of the time covered by this case study, they would have traded as ARC.)

The process

The end of the 'first phase' implementing electronic invoicing was greeted by David Oatley, Systems Manager for Hanson Aggregates Central, as follows:

> HUSSAR!!! and all that stuff. To an accompaniment of resounding cheers and popping champagne corks, on Monday 13th November 1996, we received our first 13(!) live invoices from Blue Circle Cement. Well, actually, they were processed through our purchase invoice processing system quite quietly in an overnight batch routine, and a confirmation report was waiting the following morning. However, we felt the event was certainly worthy of celebration, for it represented the culmination of over twelve months effort and involvement with CITE, Harbinger and our partners Blue Circle.

To keep things in perspective and to wind back the tape a little, the process had started with the agreement of a number of contractors and suppliers to 'make electronic information exchange happen'. Collaboration was a key element in a process that was intended to provide as much of a turn-key solution as possible.

Hanson's first involvement with EDI began in the early 1990s when initial pilot schemes were developed (one of which was with Blue Circle Cement). Sadly, due to company reorganizations, with which we are all familiar, these schemes died or were at least consigned to the 'pending tray'. Several of Hanson's customers and suppliers had again contacted them with a view to establishing EDI partnerships – some even dangling the threat of removal from tender lists. The emergence of the CITE initiative provided the catalyst to reactivate the project.

Within six months the data exchange standard had been agreed and documented. This was defined as a true subset of the international UN/EDIFACT standard, controlled under the United Nations and the International Standards Organization (ISO). By adopting a true subset (i.e. adhering to the syntax rules) it would be possible to trade across industry sectors, as well as internationally, using the same electronic format.

Having agreed the standard, the next step was to install the data exchange software and network services. A group of contractors (or whatever the collective noun is for contractors!) had negotiated with a number of EDI software and network providers. The result had been that Harbinger, a relative newcomer to the UK, was asked to provide a solution for the contractors which, understandably, was adopted by others involved in the initiative.

For reasons largely of economics, the Harbinger PC software, written to run under DOS, was chosen. With a price tag under £1000, this was an affordable solution, especially as the process still had to be proven. Coincidentally, as time has gone on, most companies have gone the same way. Even those, like Hanson, whose applications ran on mainframe computers, it was possible to transfer files to and from the PC. It was also noted that this provided a degree of comfort for operational staff as the EDI components clearly sat in their own box, isolated from the main operating systems – a kind of data exchange fire wall.

Initial problems were encountered due to the fact that the software had not been specifically designed to suit British methods of doing business. The UK Customs and Excise rules require a supplemental message to be exchanged with each batch of electronic invoices (in spite of the fact that you don't send such a message with paper invoices!) which is used to confirm the correct transmission of the data. This functionality was written into the Harbinger software, as were other specific options that had been requested by CITE. This caused some initial delays but resulted in a product geared up to operate more closely to the requirements of the construction industry.

Obviously, testing a newly released software product makes it likely that you are going to encounter bugs, and the Hanson experience was no exception. The Harbinger support team worked hard at fixing them, finding work-rounds or reporting them to their parent company in the USA. The cycle of testing, fixing and installing new versions finally came to an end and Hanson, and others, had a compliant piece of software. As Hanson was to be one of the first installations for the Harbinger system, it was arranged for a Harbinger engineer to phone them and monitor the process with them. However, so eager was the Hanson PC Support Engineer to get things going that he had already loaded the software on the designated PC and would have set up the network connection had someone not restrained him.

The next stage in the process was to write an interface to integrate electronic invoices with their accounts package, CODA. For Hanson to integrate the invoices with their software required a conversion (mapping) between the EDIFACT exchange format and a flat file. This is quite common as the transfer format is designed to be compacted and is therefore very rules based. Software finds it easier to write to/from something like a flat file, where the data content is consistently located at known positions. The CITE approach was to provide a routine that could map data between these two formats, and for both to be standardized. Initially Harbinger had provided a mapping for CITE invoices. However, as more messages were developed it was decided to adopt an independent mapping capability (using the TSI Mercator software) which can be run with different EDI software and on different operating platforms. Hanson used a

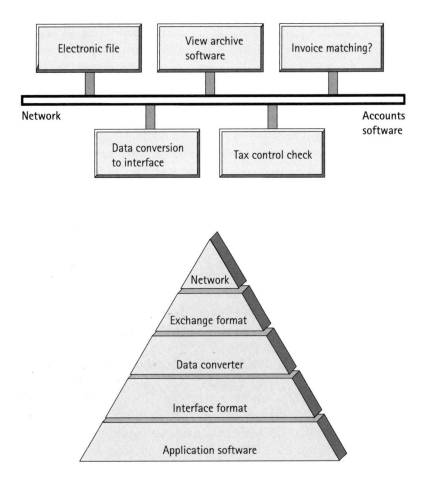

Figure 4.7 Electronic invoice receipt: information flow and process elements

DOS version of the software so that this could be automated using schedulers provided within the Harbinger software. The schedulers allow the collecting, sending and processing of electronic information to be controlled. As the scheduler can also trigger 'batch files' (i.e. files which contain software commands), almost any process can be set up to run without manual intervention. The result is that EDI software often chugs away quietly in the corner with the screen turned off.

The first plan had been to send invoices to a number of contractors (*Figure 4.7*). With this in mind Hanson wrote an outbound interface for their accounting system that would produce a flat file of sales invoices. However, about half way through the year it became apparent that delays with the contractors' internal developments meant they were not going to be in a position to make the live link as quickly as was initially envisaged. Consequently, Hanson switched resources to developing the links to their purchase order system so that they could receive invoices from suppliers. This had the additional advantage that a number of Hanson's suppliers had already implemented electronic trading systems with builder's merchants, etc.

The approach

The approach adopted by Hanson was based on a belief in the benefits of electronic exchange. Initial attempts to get EDI going had failed for reasons unconnected with the technology and more to do with commercial and operational concerns. The emergence of a collaborative industry-wide approach clearly made a big difference, but Hanson had not made this a prerequisite. However, Hanson has actively supported the idea of common exchange standards as offering the best chance for widespread adoption of EIE.

The initial contact had been made between Hanson Aggregates and a number of contractors. This offered clear commercial, as well as operational, benefits to Hanson, and had been their first priority. It was regrettable that the contractors were not as fast to get up and running as the suppliers, but they too are now increasingly 'going live'.

Having implemented the first invoice link with a supplier, Hanson then targeted similar organizations. Thus, within only a few months, Rugby and Castle Cement joined Blue Circle in sending CITE invoices to Hanson. This confirmed the analogy to the telephone such that, once you have an electronic trading link, you only need to know the number of other companies so enabled to start trading with them in the same way. However painful the first implementation may turn out to be, it is plain sailing thereafter.

The next logical expansion was to transfer the functionality developed by Hanson Aggregates Central directly to Hanson Aggregates South. A case study based on the second implementation would have filled perhaps a single paragraph, as the preparation work had already been done. The good news for this case study is that Hanson Aggregates South undertook a detailed analysis of the tangible benefits, which clearly apply to their central region as well.

There are two key targets for the next stage of the process:

- implementing electronic trading with contractors
- introducing new electronic documents, such as orders, despatch advice, etc.

In both cases, progress has already been made and their only intention is to increase the impact of electronic exchange. According to David Oatley, the key lesson they learned was 'persistence'.

The benefits

The obvious benefits of EIE are generally well known, including the ability to:

- avoid re-keying or scanning of data
- avoid transcription errors
- access data more quickly
- store and retrieve information electronically
- gain more time for planning and problem-solving.

In Hanson's case, these benefits were all very apparent. They also focused particularly on the number of tasks involved in the handling of paper invoices and registering them into their accounts system. From collecting and opening the envelopes to attaching accounts slips and preparing to match data, nine tasks were identified, timed

---

Box 4.1 Invoice receipt manual processing analysis

Nine manual tasks identified by Hanson aggregates:

1. Collection and opening of the envelopes
2. Date stamp each document
3. Count and record documents
4. Check order number on invoices
5. Separate invoices by location
6. Register invoices into the computer
7. Stamp as 'registered' and attach slip
8. Re-envelope and post to region, or store locally
9. Attach tickets and prepare for order matching

With less than 10% of invoices converted to electronic exchange ...

Time saved: over 4 person-days per month
Cost saving per invoice: 40 pence per invoice (plus 'intangible' benefits)

---

and costed (*Box 4.1*). At the time the calculations were made, around 600 invoices a month were being received electronically each month. This represented less than 10% of their total invoice processing, and so the potential growth of the benefits identified was considerable. Time saved from processing invoices amounted to just over 4 person-days each month, representing a cost saving of over 40 pence per invoice.

The intangible benefits are expected to outweigh the tangible ones, but are often discounted as being either 'woolly' or 'overstated'. Their inclusion here could be seen by some to be 'leading the witness', simply because they have not, or cannot, be analysed as can tangible benefits. However, Hanson and others who have adopted electronic exchange have largely become involved because of such benefits:

- Business partnering is strengthened by electronic exchange. Process effectiveness and mutual trust often come hand in hand. Sending invoices in an envelope is one thing; knowing that they are received and rapidly processed, without errors, is another.

- Reducing the number of transcription based mistakes must be worth something, but unless the cost of handling current problems is known, how can we value their avoidance?
- Saving time from re-keying data leaves more time to handle queries and problems that arise.
- With process automation and streamlining data matching can be achieved faster, allowing most transactions to be processed automatically; only those failing to meet specified criteria are presented for manual intervention.

Management issues

As time has gone on, and experience has been gained, implementing electronic exchange has become largely routine. The excitement of being at the forefront has diminished, but the confidence in a speedy and successful outcome is probably a fair compensation. From Hanson's perspective, they had no doubt that allocating one of their system developers to work full time on the project was crucial, especially as we needed Harbinger to develop areas, such as the multidivisional processing, which involved them in testing.

Hanson also benefited from the design of their existing computer systems. The sales invoicing processing system lent itself to generating a file of invoice information, which was then fairly easily reformatted into the CITE flat-file layout. Pre-existing programs used on the purchase side (which processed invoices passed between regions) were adapted to read-in the CITE files. Finally, they were already familiar with transferring files between their mainframe and PCs, and all these factors enabled them to immediately integrate electronic exchange with existing systems, and pass on that benefit directly to customers, suppliers and their own regional offices. Hanson's Purchase Ledger departments have adopted the concept of EDI enthusiastically now that they can see it happening 'for real', and they are now engaged with other suppliers to set up similar trading partnerships.

The cost of setting up an invoice exchange capability will vary from company to company, but the Hanson experience contains many typical elements. A point to note straight away is that, once established, an electronic exchange system can be used for many more trading partners as well as more document types, with little or no extra set-up costs. Running costs related to the software should remain the same, though transmission costs will increase proportionally.

Cost example. (All costs are based on charges in May 1999 applicable to a member of CITE and are subject to VAT at the prevailing rate.) It is expected that, with the increase functionality required to support Internet options that the cost of data exchange and mapping software could well increase in the short term. This would reverse the previously downward price trend experienced that occurred as EDI

EDI system		
1. Harbinger EDI software (CITE version)	£995	
Annual support		£405
2. Harbinger network (charge for sending/	£0	£240
receiving data)		(from)
3. TSI Mercator Mapping (conversion) software	£215	
Annual support		£60
4. CITE data converters ('maps') (free to CITE	£0	
members)		
5. CITE invoice processing software £250		
(view, print, archive)		
Total	£1445*	£720
		(from)
Hardware and internal costs		
6. PC (if none available)	£750	
7. Modem	£50	
8. System integration	See text	
* Plus optional installation support.		

became more widespread. In time, prices should again fall, though there will then be the next 'new thing' to buy!

System integration is the 'final link'. The ability to create the required file output or to import data will depend on the particular software being used. Increasingly, standard interfaces (such as those supported under the CITE initiative) are being sought as default product features. Support from software providers is starting to make this objective a reality, but this is not yet a universal opportunity. Hanson estimated their internal software integration costs ran to £8000, underlining the value of providing common solutions within packaged applications.

4.2.3 Electronic orders

As someone once pointed out to me: 'Often more cost is incurred processing order queries than our buyer ever saved ... even on his good days! ... and then there are the critical path costs that are incurred when the supply related problems occur during the construction phase of the project'. This is no criticism of buyers – without their savings, things would have been worse. The point is that cost-reduction opportunities are mostly found buried within processes and not sat staring at us on the surface.

Order exchange case study

During early 1999, Northumberland County Council (NCC) entered into a contract whereby Colas was to undertake general road maintenance work within the county. Previously this work had been carried out by the contracting division of the Council and so the changeover also required administrative systems to be implemented to manage an external service contractor. Around 20 works orders would be generated each week, some covering activities running over several months.

To support the administration of the contract, NCC decided to implement the electronic exchange of works orders using the internationally based CITE standard. As a result, both Colas and NCC would need to provide an electronic interface between their different computer applications. When the contract was awarded, neither party had the required electronic exchange services in place. With only about two months to the commencement of live exchange, this would be a good test for the implementation of CITE exchange.

Both parties adopted the basic software elements, as described earlier in the electronic invoice exchange case study. NCC modified a file output from their works order system which complied with the CITE interface format. Colas would receive and process the order from the electronic data. A small number of minor system configuration changes had to be made by NCC to comply with the defined list of codes for 'units of measure' and to break large text descriptors into field-sized elements compatible with the exchange standard.

The electronic exchange software was initially installed and tested within both organizations, in each case within a day, including operator training. For Colas, this then had to be relocated to their new offices in Newcastle, where further training also took place. NCC, as the originator of the order, created an output file written to a simple file format (fixed length field flat file) that had been specified by CITE for this purpose. This is much the same as for creating a new print file. Once this had been achieved, everything else was available 'off the shelf'. The flat file was first 'mapped' (converted) into the transfer format using a proprietary piece of software (Mercator software, TSI). The resultant file was then sent across a value added network (Harbinger) to Colas. The process for Colas was basically the same, but run in reverse. They downloaded the file from the network, converted it into the flat file and then entered the data into their order-processing software.

Evaluating the benefits from electronic exchange was difficult to quantify as previously these orders were not sent to an external organization. One clear benefit is that a formerly internal transaction has become an external order management operation without imposing many of the traditional administrative burdens. To reduce further the administration of these orders, an electronic valuation exchange was also implemented, as described in the next section.

4.2.4 Electronic valuations

Payment for the work carried out by Colas (see the previous section) would be made by the Highways Authority. However, the invoice amount had to be agreed by NCC before Colas could submit their invoice. As one invoice period involved monitoring many work orders, it would be necessary to agree how much progress had been made against each item. Further still, the figures agreed for payment in one period would set the basing point for subsequent payments. It was therefore necessary to provide a mechanism for reporting progress and maintaining common records. Such a mechanism would also provide an authorization for invoicing purposes.

The solution proposed was to exchange valuation details within an electronic file. The exchange valuation data could follow a face-to-face meeting, or simply be submitted by e-mail to NCC. Either way, NCC could accept, reject or modify the claimed amounts and discuss this with Colas until they arrived at, and authorized, the final total.

At a practical level, the CITE standard together with a basic valuation exchange software application (developed by CITE) was selected to provide the front-end contact point for the exchange of valuation data. When Colas receives the work order, individual items are transferred into a valuation file. This forms the basis of subsequent exchange and provides a list against which progress can be reported. The standard allows Colas to claim an amount of work completed based on a percentage of the total, a number items or a lump sum amount. They are also able to claim a different 'charge per item' where they believe this is justified or where it has been agreed. Perhaps not surprisingly, NCC is also able to refute all such claims and authorize payment based on their own measure of progress and item costs.

Finally, within the electronic file, NCC can return an 'authorization' code to Colas which is then quoted on the invoice submitted to the Highways Agency. As for disputes, these can be reviewed before the invoice total is agreed, or the approved claim can be accepted, leaving any re-valuation debates to be tackled before the next valuation claim.

4.3 The New South Wales initiative

In April 1998, the New South Wales (NSW) Government in Australia issued a discussion paper[12] in which they set out a strategy by which they would gain significant benefits within construction projects from new information technology. Like the UK Government, the NSW Government is the largest construction industry client in its region. They intended to get better value for money on projects ranging from hospitals to road schemes and everything in between.

Their concern was that if the Australian construction industry failed to invest in information technology, higher construction costs relative to world standards would lead to loss of market share for Australian companies, at home and abroad. In a supporting document, Bill Legg, Chief Information Officer for Lend Lease Property Services, said:[13]

> If our industry doesn't develop new systems like these (automated electronic information exchange and work-flow control) the international firms that are will sweep through Australia. Take Singapore, they only accept Building Applications and Development Applications electronically. People are always reluctant to change. But if we don't our industry will be left behind.

The strategy has three tiers:

* making greater use of information in electronic form
* establishing electronic information databases
* managing projects using the databases, supported by communication technology and electronic information at all industry levels.

All three tiers acknowledge the vital need to exploit EIE.

The clear message was that the NSW Government was going to show the way forward. Indeed, it was going to use its position as a major client to force the industry to adopt electronic information technology. In future, to win NSW Government contracts, construction companies will have to be capable of doing business electronically. Amen!

5

The role of the Internet

Recent research by the Yankee Group indicates that the Internet commerce market will grow more than 18 times in the three years up to 2001.[14]

5.1 A sense of perspective

There is no shortage of comment on the growth and commercial impact of the Internet. In this chapter, my intention is to put the role played by the Internet, relating to electronic information exchange, into the correct context. Simply put, the Internet radically alters the access that businesses, and individuals, have to global exchange capabilities. What we must not do is to confuse the means of communication provided by the Internet with the means of integration. Integration is provided by computer applications and interchange standards. In the same way, the telephone allows me to speak to people all over the world but it does not mean I will understand a word they are saying! Heather Stark, Principal Consultant with Ovam Ltd put it like this:[14]

> The Internet is like the telephone. You can't just plug it in and expect a business return. ... What distinguishes one company from another are the systems, the people and the business models which support the connection.

Connecting to a World Wide Web (WWW) service allows us to access a computer application from almost anywhere in the world. This is a tremendous business enabler, but we need to remember that this is still a manual interface. The impressive and user-friendly nature of a WWW site does not change this fact. This is not a criticism, just a statement of fact.

There are always exceptions to blanket statements and, in this case, it could be where a WWW site includes a file download containing structured information conforming to a recognized standard. Web-based electronic information interchange options are being developed that increasingly add to the range of options available to companies wishing the integrate their business processes with those of their customers and suppliers. The following comment made by Andy Ford (Vice President, Foresight) shows how even the WWW can encourage the growth of electronic data interchange (EDI) applications:[15]

> It must be pointed out that it is Web EDI, not Internet e-mail EDI, which addresses the SME problem [low penetration of traditional EDI]. Web EDI allows the SME to complete browser-based electronic forms which are converted into EDI at the Web site. The electronic form they send and receive from the Web requires no EDI knowledge and no training. If required, the Web forms system can also import and export data to eliminate key entering information and enable computer application interfacing.

As discussed later in this chapter, we must see the Internet as being 'an extension' to the ways in which electronic data can be exchanged, and not an alternative to existing technology. The global access, low-cost connectivity and flexible user interfacing provided by the

Internet profoundly impact on the way businesses and individuals interact with one another. There can be little argument that the Internet has done more than anything else to extend the benefits of electronic information exchange (EIE) to the majority of businesses and individual users. Much of what the Internet has provided was not realistically available before it emerged onto the stage. Services, such as universal e-mail and interactive WWW information sites, were simply not sustainable without the Internet.

However, we must avoid devaluing or, worse still, ignoring, the other exchange options that don't come with an Internet tag. The Internet still has a lot of growing up to do and, while it does, other exchange options will continue to provide a solid basis for business partnering and systems integration. The Internet may become as ubiquitous as the phone network as the means of data transfer and, some say, voice communications. However, experience has shown that a single solution seldom meets the multiplicity of commercial, or personal, needs.

Having sought to keep a sense of perspective about the Internet, let us not forget to consider the limitations of life before its arrival:[15]

> Although EDI has been a success for many large companies, it is estimated that EDI capable large companies have only been able to reach 20 to 40 per cent of their potential trading base.

Having just completed the first release of an exchange standard for tender documents, it was suggested to me that 'others' could have come up with a better solution. They were quite possibly right, but the fact was no one had done so over the preceding five years. In the same way, I believe that criticising the Internet is misplaced.

Traditional data exchange across value added networks (VANs) increasingly became a low-cost and accessible business tool, but its penetration failed to reach the majority of businesses. Such data exchange methods have never really been seen as the ultimate solution for small company business integration but, thanks to the Internet, the options to reach all businesses is a realistic goal.

An article in the magazine *Webmaster* made the following comment with reference to the Retail sector:[16]

> Whilst EDI has been used in a wide range of industries for several years now, it has predominantly been the domain of major players. This has left the smaller players frustrated and to a large degree out in the cold.

Though I wish this statement was not true, and even believe it did not need to be so, it is nevertheless hard to argue with. The article goes on to show how a balance between traditional and Internet exchange has been adopted. For example, it refers to an Internet trading service which had been developed to provide simple access for small companies, who required only a PC with Internet capabilities. Companies already using EDI were to be linked to the system via their traditional VANs. Considering the stance of the larger companies, I would suggest three reasons why they would do this rather than connect through the Internet:

- the Internet service was not seen to provide commercial benefits to these companies over and above those already enjoyed using a VAN
- the 'value added' services from the VAN included options for Internet services, thus preventing their users from fears they could become 'locked in'
- there were concerns as to the security of the Internet when compared with an existing, presumably trusted, approach.

In the case covered by the article, the most likely answer is the first of these suggestions, with a dose of the third point to provide extra comfort to the decision-maker. The second point is increasingly becoming the case as network providers respond to the growth in Internet activity. The service reputation of a major VAN as a trusted third party would weigh heavily in the evaluation of risks and benefits. It may also be that those companies with existing data exchange systems didn't want the problems associated with a changeover. This is bound to be a factor, but I doubt this was the sole reason. Given their data exchange experience, such companies would, had they so wished, have been well placed to transfer to the Internet option, especially if it would save them time and money. However, a move to the Internet would probably have impacted on established system automation and possibly increased the manual input required to process these documents. In other words, the Internet service had provided a way forward for many companies previously not trading electronically, while not being the only valid solution for the data communications within this trading community.

5.2 The true power of the Internet

Just as the term 'electronic data interchange' (EDI) has begun to mean different things to different people, so has the term 'Internet'. The Internet is a global communications infrastructure that provides multiple routing options for data flow between any two connected nodes. What people often talk about as being the Internet is, in fact, an Internet-based service, such as the WWW.

Electronic commerce across the Internet has been made user-friendly by the graphical interface options provided by WWW technology. The Internet itself is just the carrier of data from point to point. The true power of the Internet is that it connects a seemingly endless number of computers together regardless of location. Weeb portals, or gateways, allow information and business applications to be accessed centrally on the Internet. This makes it a truly global business opportunity which, in turn, means that commercial software providers find it highly attractive to develop services to use the Internet.

5.3 An extra, not an alternative!

Therefore, the Internet is an added extra, not a mutually exclusive alternative solution to EIE. The Internet provides a new and highly significant range of data exchange opportunities. It has opened up so many exciting new opportunities using services operating across the Internet that we are in danger of assuming everything to do with data exchange should go this way. Private networks, leased lines, VANs, dial-up modems and even disk or tape media will all continue to offer a viable means of data exchange within the vast and diverse world of business.

To help make this point, let's consider an example where an Internet-based Web service is unlikely to be the best alternative. A concrete batching plant uses automatic hopper sensors to detect when more cement needs to be ordered. When the cement level falls to a predetermined value an automated system generates and transmits an order for the next cement delivery. The order is created and transmitted without the need for any manual intervention. It would be less than efficient for someone to connect to the supplier's Web site and manually enter the order details. In this case, direct system-to-system information exchange is the obvious solution. However intuitive or attractive the cement supplier's Web site may be, it adds nothing to a process that can operate by a direct link between two applications.

Internet systems are becoming cleverer year on year, but it is time consuming to have to visit a WWW site to enter your order information on line or check product prices and availability when these data could be updated automatically by file transfer, or across a direct link between your system and that of your trading partner.

Too many people have indicated that they can see the day when they will place all their orders through the growing number of suppliers' WWW sites on the Internet. For some this may be true, but for most it would quickly consume an unacceptable amount of staff time, with few internal gains. Most businesses will adopt a range of data exchange options, each particularly suited to the specific task. Adopting a single approach would be a bit like saying that flying is so agreeable that you see no need for cars, trains and buses. The Internet is a wonderful addition to the world of EIE, but it would be a mistake to believe that businesses are best served by focusing purely on this option.

Figure 5.1 Data interfacing

5.4 Industry Internet exchange standards

The industry data exchange standards developed under the Construction Industry Trading Electronically (CITE) initiative have all recognized the potential impact of the Internet. All CITE standards include an Internet exchange option. Some have been primarily developed for Internet exchange. In several cases, the preferred data format readily suited Internet-based transfer. Perhaps these standards will migrate to XML format in the future, but there is no barrier to Internet exchange using existing standards today. Exchange could be an e-mail attachment, a file transfer or a file download from a Web site. For these documents, as surely with others to come, it was always envisaged that Internet exchange would be the user preference. Data can be transferred in many ways, the issue is which method delivers the greatest commercial advantage.

With trading documents though, it was decided to adopt the well designed, tried and tested international data standards provided by Electronic Data Interchange for Administration, Commerce and Transport (EDIFACT). Getting an EDIFACT file out of, or into, software is a specialist, often expensive, activity. Therefore a simpler interface format is normally adopted, with a data converter linking the interface and exchange formats. To facilitate this, those involved in the CITE initiative agreed to define both the exchange and the interface formats. Further still, a simple conversion routine to switch between the two was made available. It may sound unnecessarily complicated to go through two formats, but it is no different to accepting that we talk to our telephone using the spoken word and not in digital beeps. The phone is analogous with the application that converts our voices into and out of the exchange standard. The other benefit was that the interface formats could themselves be readily exchanged across the Internet (*Figure 5.1*).

Having the two data formats made it simpler, and thus probably affordable, for companies to link their applications using the EDIFACT standard. The data transfer was initially achieved using a VAN with some via the Internet. This early use of the trading standards was predominantly by the larger companies, and their decision to use a VAN was probably influenced by the following factors:

• they were exchanging large batches of repetitive documents, not single items
• traditional methods supported process automation and transfer auditing
• Internet security was still a cause for concern
• HM Customs and Excise required a transmission check document for EDI invoices which has a ready-made EDIFACT solution.

5.5 Extensible markup language

As a concept, the extensible markup language (XML) is intended to provide a data format that can be applied across the spectrum of exchange scenarios. Ultimately, XML should be as suited to presenting structured information on a Web site as it is to transferring bulk data between applications. The key word in the name is 'extensible'. XML can be customized by the user to support a wide range of business applications. Extra data tags (identifiers) can be defined specifically to suit a particular situation. Within an XML exchange, the data structure and the way in which it is to be presented and applied can all be conveyed independently. This all sounds very good, but where did XML come from and how do we deal with so much user-controlled flexibility?

XML has been developed by the WWW Consortium (W3C) to enable the open exchange of documents, including structured data elements. As more companies became connected to the Internet the need for a common data language became apparent. XML was developed so that structured data could be exchanged across the Internet

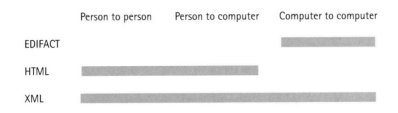

Figure 5.2 Application of data standards

in human readable form while also enabling direct application interfaces to be provided (*Figure 5.2*). The interest to industry is that we must understand how this can be exploited to support our information exchange objectives. In fact, XML is already one of the message standards being used by the CITE initiative.

Like hypertext markup language (HTML), XML is based on SGML (standard generalized markup language). To set this in some context, HTML has been used to define and control the appearance of Web pages whereas XML defines and controls the data relationships. Therefore, HTML would assign tags to information such as <BOLD>, <LEFT>, <FONT>, <COLOR>, etc., whereas with XML you could use tags such as <NAME>, <PHONE NUMBER>, <PRICE>, etc. In fact, whereas HTML defines tags, XML allows you to define tags for the data elements. This provides total flexibility, but raises a significant interoperability issue.

XML is not a replacement for HTML, rather it is a further addition to the armoury of a technology that is increasingly supporting global application integration. XML complements HTML such that we should expect documents to be accessed on a Web site with all the presentation finesse we have come to expect, but with a data content that can be directly applied within our business applications. For example, product information could be presented with pictures and catchy graphics alongside price data that could update your procurement databases and provide an object definition you could insert into a computer aided design (CAD) application. The visual representation of XML is provided using style sheets which, as if we hadn't already had enough acronyms in this section, are written using the XML style-sheet language known as XSL (extensible stylesheet language).

5.4.1 A note of caution

Despite all the benefits afforded by XML, a note of caution must be sounded. I have no doubt that XML will increasingly be used to support EIE in the construction industry, but there is much work still to be done. As mentioned earlier, XML does not impose data tag definitions. Anyone who has integrated third-party data into an application will know that flexibility is the last thing you want. Flexible in definition, yes. Flexible in application, no thanks. If your database uses a field called <PRICE>, to receive a message where this element is called <UNIT COST> would prevent data import. The tags must be agreed in advance, as should the definitions of how one element relates to another. For example, do you apply the volume discount before or after the delivery surcharge?

5.4.2 Creating an XML message

This requires a common understanding of the data structure and tag names that will be used. This is provided using what is called a document type definition (DTD) or schema (a schema is a more flexible version of a DTD, and is predicted to become the standard structure reference file). To make sense of an XML message, both parties must exchange the DTD. Put simply, XML is not an exchange standard without a DTD to define its structure.

Q: Hang on a minute, didn't we spend years defining all these data structures?

A: Why, yes we did ... the EDIFACT messages are perhaps the best example.

Q: Then why are we going down the XML road?

A: Because XML works seamlessly in the world of Internet/Web technology.

Q: But couldn't we apply the EDIFACT structures to XML?

A: Hey, you're getting good at this!

Since the emergence of XML, there have been a number of projects looking at XML/EDI opportunities (see Appendix 3). These can fast track the agreement of XML structures and tagging rules without which XML is limited to little more than a good way to send data for screen readability. One such project, called XCAT, was undertaken by a Danish consortium.[17] XCAT set out to evaluate the value of XML and to see how readily the document structures defined by EDIFACT standards could be translated into XML. Using the product information standard called PRICAT, a pilot was developed to define the XML components and to provide a translation routine to convert between the two formats. The project took about three months and proved that it was indeed possible to port EDIFACT into XML. It also raised a number of other issues, including cultural barriers and the need to decide whether backward compatibility has to be maintained once having established the XML standard. The general findings from this project are provided in Appendix 4.

There are many scenarios for this, but I would like to take two to emphasize that the solutions will depend on circumstances:

- *Scenario 1.* An established, EDIFACT-based, electronic trading community wants to extend its reach to smaller companies that, perhaps due to their size, have not become involved. Those already trading see no current need to adopt an XML approach for themselves, but would like to include more companies in the community. Making the assumption that most, if not all, of these smaller companies would have (or would buy into) an Internet connection, a translation could be developed to link the EDIFACT and XML formats. The XML messages could be received, viewed and processed (perhaps manually by some) by the smaller trading partners. For the established companies, this option may realistically enable them to achieve 100% electronic exchange.

- *Scenario 2*. An industry sector wants to establish the electronic exchange of product information. Recognizing that the Web will play a key role in such exchange, they decide to adopt an XML option. Given that there is an established EDIFACT message, this is used to set the rules for the XML standard and a conversion routine between the two formats is developed. However, new options may come along to enrich the product data exchange which are beyond the scope of the 'parent' EDIFACT message. Therefore a decision would need to be taken not to retain a backwardly compatible link to the EDIFACT message or not. In this case it may be better to use the EDIFACT message to help create an initial XML format, and thereafter to only modify the XML format.

International groups have been established by intersted parties to provide XML solutions, e.g. schemas and style sheets. For the architecture, engineering and construction (AEC) industries, aecXML is just such a development. Its ability to gain majority support and to provide universally available schemas will be essential to achieve widespread adoption. Other services, such as Microsoft Biztalk, store DTDs and schemas which can be downloaded and applied.

Commercial support for XML has been strong amongst the key players such as Microsoft, Oracle and Sun Microsystems. XML needs such cooperation to succeed as there is much work to be done if the promise is to be delivered. XML, like many exchange developments that preceded it, is not a panacea. It will have its strengths and weaknesses and will rely on the development and adoption of XML-based applications. The arrival of the Internet has revolutionized the opportunities for EIE and brought all companies in reach of each other. The emergence of XML will hopefully provide the model by which business applications can achieve full interoperability across the Internet.

6

An appointment with inertia

In a world where nothing ever stands still, inertia has to be seen as synonymous with decline.

Having sought to help construction companies to benefit from electronic information exchange (EIE) over several years, I have come to understand many more of the concerns that are genuinely held by most decision-makers. It is often falsely implied that these decision makers don't want change as, in my experience, they are all looking to improve business practices. However unexpected or irrelevant a concern may appear to be, if it is not tackled and resolved, it simply becomes an even bigger issue.

In this chapter some typical causes of inertia are discussed with the intention being to help others to identify and neutralize unjustifiable inertia wherever and whenever this is encountered.

6.1 Implementers' armour

> Too many good ideas fail to see the light of day simply because their advocates fail to recognize that resistance is seldom based on the facts of the case.

From the perspective of the construction industry, it is normally the implementers of technology-based change who can lay claim to being 'leading edge' rather than the technology itself. The battles to be fought and won by those seeking to deliver change to the business processes are primarily cultural in nature. As a direct result, it is as essential to recognize that the battleground will often be based on emotions rather than evidence. Unless innovators are ready and able to tackle this dimension, inertia can often win the day, even when the odds are stacked in favour of change.

EIE has many of the typical characteristics of an innovation likely to engender scepticism and resistance within an organization. EIE uses technology, impacts on current business processes and makes claims of 'significant' benefits. Resistance is likely to take the form of a reminder that technology is always overhyped, business-process change is always more complex than predicted and the benefits always exaggerated. The trap is to deny these points when we know they have substance. The real opposition is more likely to come from insufficient awareness of how EIE works in practice. There are few absolute answers to the repost and so arguing against such points would only give an impression that we have a blind faith in EIE and little experience of business realities.

The real battle must be fought on the commercial impact of EIE, for example:

- Can our business compete effectively if we continue to re-key all data?
- How important is supply chain partnering?
- Would our staff provide a better service with less administrative responsibilities?

- Would added value improve levels of repeat business?

From here the task is to show, using practical examples, how EIE has a proven record of delivering benefits with a clear commercial impact.

6.2 Keeping up with the Jones'

There is nothing quite like a fear of being left behind to provide the necessary motivation to change. However, there is always the risk of crying wolf, which only adds to the level of inertia. The tide is now clearly moving to a point where those that have not implemented EIE will either be commercially disadvantaged or face an ever steeper climb to catch up. the justfication for change should be built on hard evidence. Up-to-date examples can readily be found in the trade press or from a relevant association such as Construction Industry Trading Electronically (CITE) or eCentre[uk].

6.3 Dear Mr Client

In the Henley Centre report on the future of the construction industry,[18] the increasing demands placed by clients on the construction industry underlined the need for changes to traditional practices:

> Clients are becoming more demanding, more expert, or both ... and they are aware of the increasing number of competitors within the industry.

> The expectation from clients that have raised their own efficiency by rethinking their business processes (is) that construction companies will do the same.

Clients will increasingly become aware, or be made aware, of the benefits they can derive from integrated project management. Until EIE becomes commonplace, those bidding for work will undoubtedly market the specific advantages they provide through their application of EIE, as compared with their competitors. One way or another, the client will come to demand or expect their share (perhaps even a bit more) of the benefits. Faster completion, lower cost, improved information, fewer problems and enhanced facilities management are all implications delivered from the effective exchange of information between the project partners.

Interestingly, many contractors have positively encouraged clients to demand EIE within a project. The reasoning is that this would level the playing field for all those bidding for the work and would mandate that the application of EIE passes down the project line. Take-up rate would clearly be ramped up and the transition would be faster and less painful. Like a tetanus injection, we appreciate the benefits, but still prefer a single jab to multiple small ones.

6.4 Can I type my order for you?

Sometimes it can be a good idea to ask someone to do the work for you.

Perhaps it is a peculiarly British phenomenon, but I believe many of us can be more concerned about moving away from traditional practices than we appear to be about improving our performance. Custom and practice requires that we follow a set sequence of events and, perhaps just as importantly, that each step is carried out by the historically designated person. This sense of order can have its advantages, as each person knows exactly what do, when to do it and how it should best be achieved. However, at the time when change is necessary, it can equally become the major barrier preventing progress. Having been taught to follow the form book, we subsequently find it difficult to see things in any other way.

When it comes to material purchasing, many would consider that it is the responsibility of the purchaser to complete and submit the order. The advent of the telephone, in combination with the supplier's understandable interest in securing the sale, has meant that a large percentage of formal documents actually pass from the supplier to the purchaser in the form of a confirmation. This very fact was perceived as a barrier to the implementation of electronic order exchange. To many, it appeared as though they would have to give up this cherished arrangement and admit that the game was up! Caught in the act of trying to cut corners, surely electronic trading would now require that the order would once again have to pass from the purchaser to the supplier. This would end the 'phone and a confirm' procedure and impose unacceptable and unjustified change.

Concern is often expressed about the imposition of traditional trading practices as a consequence of adopting electronic exchange. The new is seen to be prescriptive rather than flexible. The reality is that those who have spent the time in developing electronic messages are just as keen to make it possible to cut out unnecessary processing. Exchange standards can be used to support a wide range of practices and enable the innovative mind to be even more devious, I mean effective, than ever before.

It is perfectly acceptable, perhaps essential, to challenge traditional procedures when making such a fundamental change to business practices. It really does not matter who types the order, or for that matter the invoice, quote or despatch note, just so long as the process is neither duplicated nor inefficient. It is this drive to reduce wasted effort that should be the watchword of those responsible for implementing electronic exchange. Just as it is limiting to blindly retain historic practices, so it would be wasteful to give up hard-won process gains by reverting to perceived good practices.

Following on the example of the supplier typing their own orders, there are perhaps many good reasons for this being a preferred option in many circumstances. The exchange of an electronic order, in this case as a confirmation, is only intended to ensure that the computer systems of both parties contain the same (correct) information. The supplier is clearly well placed to confirm the details of the order and can even provide, within the message, additional information such as the manufacturer's product code numbers. This also allows the supplier to confirm, and the purchaser to check, that the order requirements have been interpreted correctly.

The two messages here are: first, not to see electronic exchange as a rigid enforcer of traditional practices; and, secondly, to be prepared to challenge the use of traditional documents. What counts is that the right information is in the right place at the right time.

6.5 I know my costs, do you know yours?

When I first went into companies to discuss electronic exchange opportunities, I sometimes appeared to argue against myself when it came to tackling the subject of cost benefits. Having set out the many ways in which companies benefit from electronic exchange, I then suggested that they may not be able to identify a specific figure for themselves and even implied that the search may be fruitless. This, quite naturally, would lead to concerns being raised as to whether these benefits really existed and perhaps, though never voiced when I was in the room, about my own business acumen.

What actually lay behind my caution was a knowledge of the many different components that impact on the cost–benefit equation. More to the point is that many of these components had probably never been assigned a value and that others depended on how well their business could exploit a new way of working. A few examples are:

- Would your estimators submit better tenders, even win more jobs, if they had more time to process each submission?
- Would clients give more business to a cost consultant who provided faster and more comprehensive bid analysis?
- Would your accounts department have anything better to do, like resolve queries or chase debtors, if they no longer spent time keying in invoice data?
- What is the value of archives that no longer require documents to be scanned and which can be searched on any data element, not just the keyed indexes?
- How much would you gain if your project manager was able to access any document (such as architects' instructions and technical queries) directly?

- What could be saved by reducing the number of lost 'proof of deliveries'?
- How much new business could you generate by trading electronically with key business partners?
- How flexible are your systems, or managers, with regard to exploiting opportunities linked to process change?

I therefore decided that two things were needed. First, a growing number of practical examples showing what happened to other companies when they adopted electronic exchange. And, secondly, a willingness to turn the traditional argument on its head. The first is a powerful motivater and, as the weight of evidence has grown, has become the primary driving force for change. The second is often needed simply to prevent us from missing the boat, and has often been cathartic to the process of management awareness. Let me try to explain what I mean by taking one example of this in practice.

A company may be considering automating its accounts payable function, thus ending the manual production of remittance documents and cheques as well as the envelope stuffing and posting operation. Then there is the impact on the procurement function as electronic invoices and orders could possibly be involved with options for data matching and simpler query resolution. And so, before too long, the list of implications has swollen impressively. It would be at about this moment that the project manager would ask the inevitable question: 'So, how much will this save me?'. In days gone by I might have replied 'Well, that's difficult as you have identified a number of intangible elements, and clearly much depends on the characteristics of your invoice to payment ratios … but clearly there will be benefits'. However, adopting principle 2, I would say: 'Well, using the electronic exchange options identified, your cost per payment should come down to £5.75. How much lower is that than your current cost?'. To date, I have not received an answer to that question. In the event that an answer was forthcoming, I knew we had the basis on which a reasonable cost analysis could be made. I also knew that this figure was reasonable and that I would explain what I had done.

Judging by the impact this sometimes has, I hereby disclaim responsibility for others who have copied this technique elsewhere in their organization.

Having raised this example, I should at least give you some actual figures for accounts payable costs. The following information was presented at a meeting I attended in London; it is a comparison of costs across a range of industries.[19] Further details are included in Chapter 8 (Section 8.6). Typical accounts payable costs will clearly vary from company to company and be influenced by the type of business being transacted. However, typical costs per payment made (incurred without electronic payment systems) ranged from £5 to £35.

Therefore, while we should do everything we can to identify cost savings and to quantify the benefits, we must not allow a genuine inability to be specific to damn us to stagnation. Very often, the capital outlay to implement electronic exchange is much lower than people had imagined. Almost certainly, the cost of being outside the world of electronic business will be higher than was imagined.

7

The nuts and bolts – establishing an information exchange capability

You will hardly need this book to inform you that there will be no value from electronic exchange without implementation. However, misguided implementations can seriously lengthen the time and money involved and reduce the benefits that will be derived. A poor implementation can also reduce internal support and restrict your ability to expand the number of electronic trading partners. This chapter reviews the nuts and bolts required in making electronic exchange happen and how specific opportunities can be grasped.

An excess of caution can be dangerous to any development process. Given the rapid global growth in electronic commerce, companies are probably better served by 'jumping in' and gaining some practical experience. The reasons for doing this may appear less well defined than would be liked, but it is better to get an early appreciation than a late shock. As with learning to swim, you could remain nervously on the side, taking some satisfaction from watching those that took the plunge splashing aimlessly about, even though they seem to be enjoying themselves. However, when everyone else has mastered this skill, you will either be unable to keep up with the others or unsure as to what part you can play in their well-established activities. The balancing consideration is that the nervous excitement experienced with any new implementation will gradually pass, but the impact of effective planning, or the lack of it, will remain. What we need is the ability to get involved, without jeopardizing future opportunities and without wasting time, money or losing the life blood of management support.

7.1 Establishing a data link to your software

Earlier in this book I referred to 'electronic data interchange (EDI) interruptus' which is where a trading partner receives electronic data but still prints it out before entering the details into their software. This delivers very little value, other than where it offers commercial gains by giving the impression of electronic exchange taking place. The real benefits come from linking data received electronically with your application software and, subsequently, from the process improvements this facilitates. Information exchange falls, not surprisingly, in the primary categories. Category one covers information coming into your operating system, and category two is electronic information being exported from your operating system which is to be conveyed electronically to your trading partners.

Given recent developments and a growing awareness of the commercial importance of electronic commerce, neither importing nor exporting data should be considered as being an unusual expectation or something that is hard to achieve. Where genuine difficulties are experienced, managers need to give time to assessing the possible impact of this problem on their business. It is no overstatement to

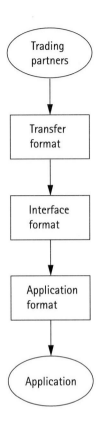

Figure 7.1 Bringing electronic data into an application. All three formats may be one and the same, but normally two will co-exist

suggest that this could restrict the company's ability to operate effectively within a relatively short timeframe.

7.1.1 Receiving electronic data

There are a number of points to consider right at the outset in order to assess how best this interface can be achieved:

- the raw data structure as received from your trading partner

- any readily available import routines available within your existing software
- what control you have over the development of the interface
- how data will be archived.

The objective is to get information into your application quickly, accurately and without manual re-keying (*Figure 7.1*). The information will arrive in one format, which may, or may not, be the same as the format you ultimately feed to your application. If not, then a conversion, through an interface format, will be used.

There is not always the need for an intermediate, or 'interface' format but, despite their apparent redundancy, they can have advantages. In an ideal world there would be one exchange format which is understood by all software. Until that is the case, we must have a strategy to sensibly resolve two issues, namely:

- the need to implement electronic exchange *now*
- the need for a solution that remains compatible with emerging technologies.

Your information exchange service (e.g. a value added network (VAN) or the Internet) and your operating software are both likely to change, even grow, over time as your business and the available technology advance. Your choice of import protocol for electronic information needs to protect your immediate and longer term business interests. As discussed in the next section, importing data through a common 'interface format' may enable you to manage component changes more simply and at lower cost in the longer term. It should be possible to change components of your system without serious impact on the individual applications that are involved in the process but are unaffected by the specific substitution.

Raw data structure

Hopefully the data you receive will adhere to a recognized exchange standard. This should always be sought as it minimizes the time and cost you will incur when establishing electronic exchange links. Be prepared to ask your trading partners to adopt such a standard, even if they are a big customer. Often companies can accommodate recognized standards, even where this may not be their first choice.

Initiatives such as Construction Industry Trading Electronically (CITE) have provided industry standards which can be readily and confidently adopted to support commercial information exchange developments. To know what the raw data will look like is a great help, to know that the same format is used by others adds a warm feeling of confidence and belonging!

Readily available import routines

The day will come when electronic exchange is as fundamental to business life as the telephone. When it does (and it won't be long), data interfacing will no longer be a matter requiring special consideration. In the meantime we have to work out how best to get electronic data into our software applications.

There is a growing number of exchange standards which, through their widespread adoption, are increasingly being supported as a standard feature within commercial software products. Such features make the adoption of fully interfaced electronic exchange about as simple as it can get. Thus, it is well worth asking your software provider whether they have provided, or would supply, an import routine for the exchange standard you wish to adopt – especially where you are not the only company that could benefit from this.

Check what format your software currently provides as a standard feature. Depending on how simple it is to provide a new import routine, linking to an established interface is likely to be an attractive option. The rules governing your application should already be enshrined in a proprietary interface, thereby increasing confidence in a successful outcome.

Where there is no import capability a little bit more detective work will be required. You will need to find out how your application stores its data and to find out how you could add new information, as though it had been entered manually. This is most likely to involve writing to the databases used by the application in question. There are also products known, so I am told, as 'key-stroke replicaters' that can be used to mimic manual key entry, but I have not heard of their use in this way over the last five years. I would therefore be hesitant to put them forward as a viable solution, but there are times when the strangely shaped spanner comes into its own!

Even when using recognized exchange standards, such as the international formats available from Electronic Data Interchange for Administration, Commerce and Transport (EDIFACT), it is often the case that we are best served by converting this into a different structure, or 'interface format', before it is entered into our software. This may sound odd, but has several advantages:

- the final input to your software can all be through a single chan-nel, even where multiple exchange formats are received
- the conversion (between transfer and import formats – called 'data mapping') may be common to an industry sector and thus may be shared by many companies (see the Section 1.7 on the CITE initiative)
- the final import routine will be simpler and cheaper to maintain
- the transfer format can be kept as compressed as possible, thus reducing transmission cost and time
- the import, conversion and transfer functions remain separate entities, allowing any one element to be changed without impacting on the others.

Progress with import options

Given that nothing ever stands still, two developments should impact on this piece of the jigsaw. First, business software will increasingly provide a ready-made interface for use with the common data exchange formats (*Figure 7.2*). Secondly, the interface format may

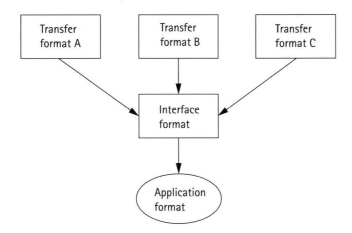

Figure 7.2 A common interface format can protect your application from multiple interface maintenance

increasingly become the transfer format, as the cost and time associated with data transfer becomes less significant a factor.

The CITE initiative is a good illustration of this point. The trading standards (enquiries, orders, invoices, etc.) have adopted the international EDIFACT standards and a conversion (data mapping) has been provided to link this to and from a simple interface format. Conversely, the tendering, valuation and project information standards adopted an exchange format that remains unchanged throughout the export/transfer and import cycle. As availability and usage increases, simplicity will become a major driving force – even an expectation.

There are many options available when considering data interface formats, but I have rarely, if ever, come across a business manager remotely interested in which one is used. From comma separated value files (CSVs) to flat files and database structures beyond, the possibilities are endless. The important point is that the data can be read into your software without difficulty. If the process cannot be made to run simply, intuitively or automatically, sceptics will still have access to the 'not yet' button.

The CITE initiative therefore adopted one interface format to be used for all trading standards, namely a flat file. To be specific, a fixed field length flat file broken into discrete segments, such as 'header', 'address' or 'price' information. Therefore, when writing an import routine, you knew exactly where to look for the data element required without needing to understand detailed syntax rules. For example, the invoice currency is always three digits long starting at character position 488 in the header segment. Hopefully, by adopting a format used by many different companies, the value to cost ratio will increase favourably. At the same time, such formats are much more likely to be provided as standard features.

Interface development control

As we have not yet reached the time when standardized data exchange is a default software feature, the ability to reprogram software remains a factor in the data exchange equation. There are three main possibilities when linking your software to the world of electronic data:

- you own the right and have the ability to program a suitable import routine
- you use commercial software that has a 'provided' import format and you are able to write your own data converter to present the data compatible with this import format
- you use commercial software but have to get the software provider to write any new interface to support electronic interchange.

For most companies, commercial software packages will provide the bedrock of their IT dependent business processes. In such cases, where a specific interface is required to enable electronic information exchange (EIE) to be achieved, the support of the software company will make a big difference. Hopefully there will be enough of their customers seeking the same interface that this will be provided as a commercial necessity, or at a greatly reduced cost when compared to a 'one-off' undertaking.

Where a company either owns or has the ability to develop their software, with this flexibility comes the need to adopt a disciplined approach. It is quite possible to use this ability to create bespoke interfaces to meet each and every new interface opportunity. At the same time, you are almost certainly committing your IT department to an increasing maintenance problem. Initially it may not appear to make sense to provide an import capability through an intermediary format. This is hardest to appreciate the first time an interface is provided, when a direct import rightly appears to be the most sensible option.

A decision has to be taken at the outset to decide whether multiple interchange standards, or exchange technologies, are likely to be required. My recommendation, for commercial safety reasons, is to assume that multiple options will be adopted. Should this assumption turn out to be wrong, the worst you will suffer is a slightly more complicated interface route. If the assumption is correct, you will be well placed to build your growing exchange portfolio through a managed interface. After all, the need to support multiple formats may simply be a result of a phased migration towards the latest 'emerging' information exchange service from that you initially adopted.

Data archives

The adoption of electronic exchange for incoming information can be a tremendous opportunity for those with large archives or who regularly go searching through archives for a particular document. The ability to store electronic documents, either separately or within an electronic document management (EDM) system, greatly improves the ability to organize and retrieve information when and where required. Security is also improved due to the loss of flammable paper storage and the ability to readily hold copies at more than one location.

The reason for raising archiving here is that this subject must to be considered as part of the data import process. It is possible to see the immediate process gains from electronic exchange and to miss the roll played by paper in information retention. Very often, only a fraction of the contents of a document will be recorded in software such as accounts, procurements, etc. Manual document processing selects and inputs the limited information, often well below 50%, into a software package. This limited data enables the software to undertake its designated tasks. The full information content, perhaps added to by a few critical notes penned by hand, is then archived for the requisite period. It was not long before the difference between processing and storing electronic data was highlighted. Archiving electronic data requires careful consideration, as it is currently the full message that has to be retained – and with a viewing facility.

How should an electronic document be stored, retrieved, viewed, annotated and even printed to meet future needs? This issue first came to light when consideration was given to the receipt of electronic invoices. Such documents have to be retained for legal and tax purposes for many years. They must also be traceable to support auditing and dispute resolution to name but two examples. The data flowing into the accounting software was clearly insufficient and comments must be able to be added and retained for future reference. The solution adopted was to produce a software product that would enable the importing, viewing, archiving and printing of invoices together with the provision of a number of locally controlled fields, including a memo field for use where a lengthy text comment is required. This was a specific solution which delivered to accounts departments a replacement to the paper archive while providing a library service for interrogating full invoice details during their initial processing. Hopefully most invoices will not be viewed this way, but at least the capability exists.

Whether such a specific solution is employed, or whether information is stored in an EDM package, consideration must be given the data format to be presented to the archive. Three main options normally arise:

- retain the original file format, as received
- retain data in the intermediate 'interface' format
- retain a specific format used by your software or EDM package.

Given that the cost of data storage is dropping all the time, there is some merit in keeping archives in more than one format, at least initially. If you are using a VAN service, you could also ask them to retain copies of your messages for an agreed period of time. This adds an extra security dimension and is seen by some to provide an independent confirmation of original data content should a dispute arise where one party is accused of altering electronic transaction records.

Where an interface format is used, retaining data in this format has merit. This presents a common archive structure, regardless of how many exchange standards are currently in use. It also precedes application entry, which should add confidence that it has not been changed by subsequent processing. Initiatives, such as CITE, can also build shared support services around an interface format, as could an EDM package.

The emergence of digital signatures and certificates will help those exchanging electronic information to confirm, for all time, the integrity of the original message contents. Though appealing, especially to those of a nervous disposition, these impose a level of security not normally applied to paper-based exchange. As such, as confidence and trust grows, such measures are likely only in exception. Conversely, it may be that their application becomes so cheap and simple that it makes it silly not to use them.

In closing this section, the key point is that at least one archive format is selected and the appropriate steps are taken to ensure that subsequent retrieval, viewing and printing can readily be achieved.

7.1.2   Sending data

Sending data is subject to many of the principles described in Section 7.1.1 above, but there are some differences to highlight. When establishing a data export capability from your software, the merit of integration is abundantly clear. Re-keying information at the receiving end is bad enough, but to consider re-keying it at the sending end should set all the alarm bells ringing.

The sending points to consider at the outset in order to assess how best this interface can be achieved are:

- the information exchange format
- any readily available export routines available within existing software
- what control you have over the development of an interface
- how data will be archived.

The objective is to get information out of your application quickly, accurately and without manual re-keying. The information will be sent in the exchange format which may, or may not, be the same as that originally exported from your application.

Information exchange format

As always, a key driver will be the information exchange format to be used between you and your trading partners. Aim to implement the minimum number possible but, at the same time, recognize that commercial and technical developments will reward those that have adopted a flexible approach. This does not mean that you benefit from adding new exchange standards as and when these are proposed by a trading partners. Such an approach does build a flexible exchange capability, but it can be unnecessarily expensive to maintain. On the contrary, I always advocated striving for the minimum number of exchange formats necessary to support commercial activities. There is a considerable difference between adopting a flexible approach and being so flexible as to always be accommodating the interests of others. As noted before, initiatives such as CITE provide industry standards which can readily and confidently be adopted to support commercial information exchange developments.

Readily available export routines

Sending electronic data should be possible even where legacy systems are involved. With older software products, or new ones without a defined data export capability, there will always be one data output – the one that supports printing. That said, I don't suggest this as a simple option, just an available one! Given the impact of the millennium bug on legacy software, it is expected that an increasing proportion of software will at least have a proprietary import and export capability on which to build a information exchange services.

Interface development control

My comments here replicate those mentioned earlier in Section 7.1.1, with perhaps one difference. When sending data, provided you can get information out of the software you then have control of the process from there on. Receiving data involves understanding how the software handles information. Sending data simply comes down to arranging it in the correct format and sending it on its way. An interface format is just as valid a consideration and provides the same blend of system protection and flexibility as when receiving data.

Data archives

Where traditional paper-based archives had been maintained for documents sent out by a company, an equivalent process must therefore be established when electronic exchange is implemented. In some instances the paper document is still produced for internal purposes. However, the availability of a paper copy should not automatically be seen as providing the logical archive format, even when scanned into a document management system.

Archives could be maintained using the electronic exchange (or interface) format, provided a viewing and printing capability is retained. Electronic document management systems should be capable of storing documents as data files and could be provided with the necessary viewing and printing capabilities to complete the loop. The objective should be to retain the ability to interrogate the archived information by searching on any field within the document. This is where electronic data files have a big advantage over scanning document images.

7.2 Establishing an electronic trading link

Increasingly this should be seen as an off-the-shelf option. When the business decision is taken to implement electronic trading, the decisions to be made should focus on the process implications and opportunities. The technology exists. Valid questions would relate to the costs, functions and availability of a particular solution, but not to its technical development or operation. We use computers with little knowledge of their operating systems, and we should use electronic exchange services in the same way. Do they do what I want at a price I can justify?

Provided a flexible interface to your software is established, my advice would always be to implement an electronic trading link at the earliest opportunity. This technology is fast moving and businesses need experience on which to base long-term strategic initiatives. On top of that, early involvement has invariably delivered operational benefits and not 'pioneer's cramp'.

Perhaps one of the key decisions is to decide which trading link will be the first you will set up. It is seldom a good idea to convert vast swathes of your business to electronic exchange all at the same time – though this could be one of the dangerous consequences for those that keep delaying implementation plans. When seeking the right place to start, or perhaps where next to go on your exchange quest, the following facts should be considered for your different trading partners, both as suppliers and customers:

- the volume of business documents exchanged (i.e. the number of documents, not their value)
- the frequency of any exchange (daily, monthly, etc.)
- the nature of the trading relationship (e.g. one-off contract or long-term partner)

- the potential impact on your own internal resources
- the potential impact on your trading partner's resources
- support from existing trading communities
- existing data exchange experience/commitment from trading partners.

Very often, evaluation of these factors highlights an unexpected trading partner, or document, that will offer the greatest value as an electronic exchange opportunity. For example:

- relationships with major suppliers may have resulted in fewer higher value orders and invoices being exchanged, whereas other suppliers may generate a higher volumes of paperwork
- some trading partners could more readily be able to implement electronic exchange, thus providing valuable impetus to the initial implementation process
- some trading partners could be responsible for a higher percentage of queries and disputes – which electronic exchange could help to prevent.

The range of practical options available is growing all the time but this is not a reason to delay implementation. Equally, each technology should not be seen to be mutually exclusive, forcing a decision as to which is the best. Just as you may walk to the park, drive to work and fly to your holiday resort, so you could send a disk to some trading partners, an e-mail file to others and have a VAN connection with still more – all at the same time. The trading link is simply a means to an end.

7.2.1 Establishing a VAN link: an introduction

VAN services predate the Internet explosion, but remain a core information exchange option. Such networks provide more than just a connection between two businesses. Over recent years, VANs have responded to the emergence of Internet technologies to broaden the value-added services they provide. Indeed, the 'traditional' VAN is hard to find, as most now provide many more services than before. Harbinger, one such global company, describe themselves as a 'provider of business-to-business electronic commerce software, services and solutions'. They go on to confirm the importance placed on growing Internet services by setting themselves the objective 'to serve more customers using Internet protocols (IP) than any other provider'.

VANs operate on highly dependable computer systems, such as tandem processors, which operate in a supported environment around the clock. Disaster recovery services are normally provided using off-site emergency backup systems to build user confidence to implement electronic exchange. Security and the integrity of business information is controlled to keep unauthorized users off these networks and to ensure that transmissions reach the desired destination.

VANs can provide more than simple data exchange. They can also host custom services, such as catalogues, broadcast messaging and message translators from one format to another, even data-to-fax conversion.

Connection to a VAN should be possible anywhere in the world. In some cases, local dial-in capabilities are provided, and Internet access will further ensure that connections can be established wherever these services are required.

It should also be noted here that the major VANs have established interconnections between themselves. This means that a company connected to one network can exchange data with a user on a different network. This helps all the network providers to deliver a comprehensive service to their users. It is a bit like the postal service where you can send a letter anywhere in the world but without your local postal service employing staff all over the world to make these deliveries.

Available VANs

Over the last few years, mergers, takeovers and service developments have all resulted in the contact details for VANs going out of date faster than fresh cream. However, the global network services that have primarily been considered within the UK construction sector to support exchange developments are:

- GE Information Services (GEIS)
- Harbinger
- British Telecommunications
- AT&T
- IBM.

GEIS took over the INS network that had supported early UK EDI developments and so hosts a number of companies that became involved during the early days.

Harbinger was little known in the UK when the construction sector set up the CITE initiative in 1995, but is now one of the largest international network providers. Harbinger was chosen as the preferred supplier by a group of contractors and, probably as a result, has been adopted by most CITE members that have come into electronic exchange for the first time subsequently.

Connecting to a VAN

Connecting to a network is basically about having the ability to send or receive data in a recognized exchange standard. The rest is much the same as for sending a parcel. Who offers the best services at the right price. Once that is decided, there is a set path to follow in setting up the service. The process is quite painless.

VAN charges. As with so many competitive services, especially where related to telecommunications, it would seem that understanding the different pricing structures can be hard work. Gradually, things are becoming simpler and connection charges cheaper. In most cases, the overall service package is the driving force, especially where the network provider has a proven track record in your business sector. Changing from one network to another is also increasingly simple to achieve and so the cost–benefit equation can be monitored over time.

Charges to look out for include:

- Connection – one-off set-up charge (becoming increasingly rare).
- Transmission – sending and/or receiving data.
- Storage – sometimes free for a standard period, but varies.
- Interconnections – Costs relating to messages sent to or received from other VANs.

Two charging examples (based on information available in 1999) are given in the box. To help make sense of these figures, a good rule of thumb is that a document, such as an invoice, is around 2.5 kilocharacters in size.

VAN software (or EDI software). Some networks provide bespoke data exchange software to manage the connection to their network. Others can be accessed from a range of 'enabled' software. Overall, this is not a significant factor, as connection to one major

Harbinger	
Joining fee	None
Monthly subscription	None
Monthly transmission	£55 (includes 1000 kilocharacters)
Transmission	Charge per additional message: none
	Charge per additional kilocharacter: 10 pence
Storage	None
GEIS	
Joining fee	£250 (£450 if using third-party software)
Monthly subscription	£87.50
Monthly transmission	£21.70 (includes 250 kilocharacters/ 25 messages)
Transmission	Charge per additional message: 21 pence
	Charge per additional kilocharacter: 6.5 pence
Storage	£2.50 per item, per day after 5 days

network gives you access, through interconnections, to the others. As with the VANs, there are several providers of EDI software, and delaying progress to undertake a lengthy evaluation of the different options can be counter-productive. There are normally a few tried and tested options available to support your particular application from which to choose. Also, careful implementation allows quick progress to be made, while knowing that the software element could be changed later. If this sounds dangerously simplistic, it is because the choice of EDI software is the data exchange equivalent of deciding if you want white self-sealing envelopes or bulk standard buff ones. It does matter, but not enough to delay posting your business documents.

EDI software, when sending data, imports your electronic documents, validates them, wraps them in an electronic envelope and sends them to the network. Receiving data is the same process in reverse. There may also be a process scheduler which can be programmed to automate everything from moving data and triggering batch files to checking your mailbox every 10 minutes. Most products come with, or support, a data mapping (conversion) function that can be used to support the interface with your software. These can be quite daunting and, where a community adopts a common standard, can lead to duplicated effort on the part of many companies. Therefore the CITE initiative decided to develop and supply data mapping functions itself so that the work could be undertaken once and then shared by all in the trading community.

Software prices. The cost of purchasing EDI software varies considerably depending on the operating platform. However, most companies have started out by implementing a PC-based solution and then uploading or downloading data to or from their main software. This keeps down the initial costs and provides a more apparent separation between your application and the world of information exchange. In time it may prove necessary to migrate to an EDI product that runs alongside your main software, but by then valuable experience and confidence will have been gained.

I used to hold the view that information exchange software, which had reduced dramatically in price through the 1980s and 1990s would continue this trend. However, I now believe that the rapid growth in exchange technology and services will lead to a short-term step up in price. Entry-level products will include far greater functionality than before, driving up prices. Prices for the next generation of PC-based software is expected to result in more products being priced nearer to the £5000 mark. Previously, PC products have been available for around £1000. Hopefully the extended capabilities of the new products will justify any extra cost.

The fall in price of Internet Web browsers, to the point that some are now free, is a model that is very unlikely to apply to business level data exchange software, as these products are not in the same competitive maelstrom. One price change that could occur is the erosion of differentials that currently exist between software for PCs and that for larger systems. With the expanded power available from PCs and PC networks, some software providers have increased the capabilities of their PC products to match those previously delivered in midrange products. As a result, the pricing of PC and midrange software products is becoming increasingly the same.

Therefore, taking the previous comments into account, the following can only be taken as guide prices:

PC software (Microsoft Windows) £500 to £5000
UNIX £3000 to £10 000
Larger systems £10 000 upwards

7.2.2 Establishing an Internet commerce link

Much confusion has arisen over the use of the Internet to support EIE developments. The confusion comes in two guises. First from a belief that Internet-based electronic exchange is different from other known other forms of exchange (e.g. VANs). Secondly, from the never ending publicity concerning new Internet developments. The role of the Internet is discussed in Chapter 5 of this book, and so I

confine myself here simply to setting out some of the options for linking business partners together using Internet services.

Internet electronic mail (e-mail)

The growth of Internet e-mail connections has provided one of the
most readily accessible options for moving data between businesses.
The e-mail message can be seen as a cover note with the data file sent
as an attachment. Increasingly this form of communication is being
adopted by businesses and is particularly suited to one-off data
exchange requirements such as those used within a short-term contract. As the data files (exchanged as e-mail attachments) almost
always require a manual intervention by the sender and receiver, this
is not a seamless link from one application to another.

Dedicated file transfer

Where files are to be transferred across the Internet on a more regular
basis, the use of the file transfer protocol (FTP) provides a more reli-
able format. FTP is particularly useful where data files are to be
transferred to, or downloaded by, multiple trading partners. Users can
set up a specific FTP site on the Internet which can be linked to a
WWW site for ease of use.

The World Wide Web

The third area I shall touch on is the World Wide Web (WWW or
Web). From a connectivity point of view of, the WWW operates on
many different levels:

- At its simplest, the WWW provides information services that
  can be viewed using a Web browser. Web browsers are software
  products designed to help users navigate around the Web, view
  Web sites and manage Web services (including viewing XML
  files, for example).

- Information can be provided in a file format to be downloaded either from the Web site or from a related FTP site.
- A Web site can host applications linked directly or indirectly to an operating system. This clearly opens up a wide range of opportunities for information services.
- A visitor to a Web site can input data manually into a screen form or, where the functionality exists, upload a file. Uploading files which can then be processed 'at the Web site' (i.e. on the computer you have connected with) expands the scope of Web-based information processing … and exchange.

To connect to all of these examples a user would normally only need access to a suitable Web browser and a connection to the Internet. The provider of the service could rent space from an Internet service provider (ISP) to host their Web pages and inclusive applications. They could, if they preferred, or the application was large enough, set themselves up with their own Web server (i.e. a Web-connected computer hosting the required applications).

Internet commerce characteristics

From an information exchange perspective it is important to differentiate between system access and data transfer. Neither an Internet connection nor an application-based Web site will, of themselves, improve your data transfer services. Consideration must always be given to how information will flow from one system into another without manual re-keying of the data.

Information flowing into or out of Internet/WWW services must adhere to the same information exchange rules as for all other transfer options:

- Provide an import/export capability for each application.
- Manage multiple data formats (interface management).
- The data structure (standard) used for the exchange.
- How will data be archived?

Summary

Connecting to the Internet to establish e-mail and Web browsing capabilities is a fundamental step that all businesses should take. However, this is just the start. Internet data exchange, like everything else, has to be defined and managed. Be prepared to challenge fashion and consider that the Internet may not always be the best option when deciding how to exchange data between you and your trading partners. It is a great way to send e-mail, check the location of a parcel delivery and to order a growing range of goods and services. It is not so obviously the link down which to send batches of invoices, payment instructions or your tax details.

The EIE activities that predated the Internet will largely continue, even expand, in the post-Internet age. The Internet will offer improvements on some pre-existing exchange services, but others will remain the best solution available to us. Therefore, we should see the Internet as adding to the range of options and not as a mutually exclusive solution. With each month that passes, new uses for the Internet will be presented to us. We must be able to separate the wheat from the chaff, but we must embrace the Internet if we are serious about EIE.

8

Specific implementation examples – the CITE initiative

8.1 Establishing an electronic trading system

As operational use has grown, a range of solutions has been established to support companies to quickly implement electronic trading. These include:

- EDI software compliant with the industry exchange standards
- value added network (VAN) services
- data exchange formats suitable for Internet-based exchange
- data mapping (conversion) to convert messages between the Electronic Data Interchange for Administration, Commerce and Transport (EDIFACT) and system interface formats
- bespoke software to support the viewing, archiving and printing of electronic trading documents.

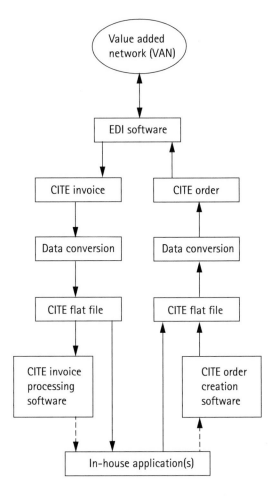

Figure 8.1 Some typical components of an electronic trading system – using a VAN

Using the example of a company sending orders and receiving invoices to set out the general principles, *Figures 8.1* and *8.2* show the main elements of an electronic trading system. In *Figure 8.1* data are transferred in the international EDIFACT format across a VAN. In

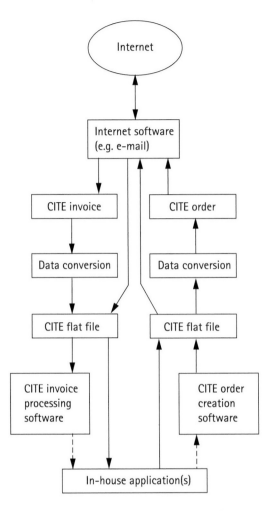

Figure 8.2 Some typical components of an electronic trading system – using the Internet. When using the Internet exchange, the data transfer could follow the dotted-line route, provided both parties can interface with the flat file format

Figure 8.2 the option of using Internet exchange is shown. In the latter case, either the EDIFACT or flat file format can be exchanged, as preferred.

8.1.1 Specific considerations – invoices

Exchanging invoices is often the first experience many companies have with electronic exchange. This is perhaps because invoices are widely used, numerous and clearly the cause of high levels of unnecessary manual handling and re-keying. However, they require specific exchange rules, set by HM Customs and Excise (see Appendix 2), and their importance tends to result in invoices being exchanged across a secure network, such as a VAN. I would therefore contest that, having implemented invoice exchange, other message types should be easier. The good news is that implementing invoice exchange itself is straightforward.

In the UK, batches of invoices sent electronically are required to be accompanied by a tax control message (TAXCON). This message handles the key requirements detailed in Appendix 2 and is used simply as a transmission check. The sender of the invoices sends a message to confirm how many invoices there are, their total value and total VAT amounts. The recipient recalculates these figures and checks them against the values reported by the sender. Both parties must print and retain a copy of this message. Provided the figures match up, the invoices can be processed. There is no need to be able trace an invoice back to the appropriate TAXCON message, the check is purely on the transmission.

A TAXCON message is not required when only a single invoice is exchanged.

UK-based companies planning to exchange electronic invoices (send or receive) must notify their local HM Customs and Excise Office of this intention at least 30 days before going live. This gives HM Customs the 'option' to come and inspect your implementation to confirm that all is as it should be. Increasingly, VAT offices are aware of electronic invoices and they are looking to promote their use. The CITE invoice standard and the tax control message were checked with HM Customs and Excise during their development.

8.2 Establishing an electronic tendering system

This is possibly the easiest option to adopt, largely because of the growing support of commercial software companies. The standard provided for the industry has been designed so that it can be used by those using word processors or spreadsheets. However, if we are to gain the full benefits of electronic tendering, we should consider how structured data exchange can link directly to functions within a proprietary system.

Given that the traditional exchange of tender documents forced a manual 'pen and ink' stage, the incentive to use proprietary systems was limited. The significant benefits available from electronic tendering clearly changes things. Much more of the process can be automated and the shorter turnaround times afforded by this technology will be exploited by clients. The result will almost certainly be that those with proprietary systems will be at an advantage.

8.2.1 Tender documents

Contractors and quantity surveyors collaborated in establishing the ability to exchange electronic tender documents. The format allows tenders to be exchanged electronically, regardless of the standard method of measurement being used, and supports multiple currency exchange if this is required. The CITE standard is increasingly included as a feature within commercial software packages, making this opportunity available to a rapidly expanding proportion of the industry.

8.2.2 Link to valuation exchange

The detailed valuation information and summary details can now be exchanged electronically. This standard links seamlessly with the bill of quantities format or can be used on its own.

8.3 Project information exchange

The many organizations involved in the construction phase of a project rely on the effective exchange, and retention, of a wide range of information. Whether it is an architect's instruction, a technical query or a transmittal note, accuracy, timeliness and an ability to quickly cross-reference to other correspondence prevents errors, unnecessary disputes and consequential delay. The CITE standard provides a comprehensive solution to the exchange of project information.

8.3.1 Approach

A single exchange format has been specified under the CITE initiative which can transfer structured information extracted from the wide range of documents exchanged between project partners during the 'on-site' phase of a project. This format can be used to import data into different software packages, giving each company the freedom to choose how they prefer to handle such communications.

8.3.2 Documents covered

The document types covered by this standard are almost endless, but have been grouped under one of five main document types as follows:

- instructions
- queries
- vouchers
- notices (and certificates)
- others.

Within each document type a specific document name is provided, such as:

- architects instructions (AI) – instruction
- clerk of works instruction (CWI) – instruction
- technical query (TQ) – queries
- final certificate (FIN) – certificate.

8.4 Goods receipt automation

We know that our well-managed procurement and accounting systems can all be found wanting at times. However, nothing torpedoes ordered management better than our apparent inability to keep despatch notes out of the mud, or to retain proof-of-delivery documents. The delays and payment disputes that normally ensue just add to the frustration, not to mention the mounting costs. There was a theory (now wholly disowned) that supply chain disputes were a healthy way to keep suppliers on their toes. The truth (now widely proclaimed by the good and the great) is that such disputes help neither side and simply hamper process improvement.

Building on the effective exchange of data provided by CITE, contractors and suppliers have worked together to find a way out of the mire. The Automation of Goods Receipt Processing standard provides a range of options that enable different operating practices to address the problem of the muddy puddle. The challenge was to build an inclusive process, to prove it operationally, to realize operational benefits and build more effective trading relationships. This objective would be achieved when material delivery ceased to be a prime initiator of payment delay and disputes.

Following early trials and operational reviews, the first full release of this standard provided a single bar-coded despatch note number on material delivery tickets. It was soon agreed that bar codes were excellent for providing structured data in paper format. However, earlier proposals for multiple bar codes had run into practical difficulties. Suppliers found it difficult to print multiple bar codes, and contractors doubted the practicalities of getting site personnel to spend the time scanning them all. It was also recognized that even with a dozen bar codes you would still not have all the data required. Thus, the single bar code option was agreed upon.

Simple for most suppliers to provide, this has delivered a readily accessible solution. More than accessible, it is surprisingly powerful in transforming many different approaches to procurement and payment management:

- the single bar code can be used as a 'key' to unlock, by association, the full data provided within an electronically transferred despatch note or invoice
- hand-held scanning technology was used to record variation data where the delivery note and physical delivery did not tie up
- data from the hand-held unit can readily (even by radio transmitter if appropriate) be uploaded to the procurement, accounting and stock control software.

This pragmatic solution could provide an accessible solution for the majority of users and offers significant benefits, especially to those engaged in supplier partnering.

However, where full despatch details are required electronically on site, this would need to be provided in advance of delivery. This is not 'normally' the case, but is one of those accepted failings we may need to challenge. For example: a 'good' despatch system should now be able to e-mail the despatch details at the same time it prints the loading note. This should end the 'accepted' belief that the electronic despatch information takes longer to arrive than the physical delivery. Despatch data could then be uploaded into the hand-held unit at the site. Then, when the bar code is scanned, the full despatch details could be accessed and verified. Any changes could be agreed and authorized – being uploaded to the accounts system and possibly being returned to the supplier. This also provides a direct link to the order and pricing information which opens further benefits for material costing and stock management.

The bar-coded despatch note will hopefully become a standard feature as it offers high returns from a low investment. Other technologies will extend the range of options, but these should not be seen as a reason not to support the bar code option. The bar code should be viewed as a basic service while other technologies are evaluated. Many companies may continue to benefit from the single bar code long after alternative technologies became operational. Some of the technology likely to be considered for application in this field includes:

- *Smart labels.* These use embedded chips that allow their data content to be read 'in proximity'. Some chips also allow data to be written to them. The cost of this technology is high, but reducing.
- *Touch memory tags.* These can store data in a portable format. Their durability, cost and simple operational characteristics make these one of the most likely technologies for use in this kind of environment.
- *Smart cards.* A different form of a touch memory tag, as used for phone cards, etc. These too can have a read/write capability.
- *RF tags.* Radiofrequency tagging.

Delivering materials to site has been described as like sending a rocket around the dark side of the moon – as you never quite know what will reappear! Together with the CITE electronic exchange of orders, despatch notes and invoices, this development provides a practical way of maintaining process visibility, reducing costly disputes and enabling processes to be streamlined.

8.5 Inland Revenue schemes

Under the new Construction Industry Scheme (CIS) launched in August 1999, contractors gained the opportunity to submit some of the payment voucher information using electronic information exchange (EIE). With all the new vouchers having to be completed and submitted on a monthly basis, the use of EIE by contractors may be the only sensible way to manage the volume of information generated by this scheme.

Having adapted operating systems to support the new scheme, the implementation of the electronic lodgement of tax information was perhaps the simplest part of the change process. It is also one of the most beneficial aspects in terms of the impact on day-to-day operations. The Inland Revenue did not implement this scheme to reduce our administrative burden but to fight tax fraud. In fairness to the

Inland Revenue, they always said the scheme would add significantly to the previous level of administration. The good news was that basis of the Inland Revenue's electronic exchange was to be the international EDIFACT data format. This was entirely in line with the approach adopted by CITE for trading documents (orders, invoices, etc.) and was therefore simple for CITE users to implement.

To ensure the implementation of the electronic exchange option was as simple and cost-effective as possible, CITE worked with the Inland Revenue to provide tangible services as well as general advice. The main deliverables were:

- a 'flat file' specification that can be used as a standard software interface by contractors
- a program (mapping) to convert the flat file into the structure required by the Inland Revenue
- support for the implementation of the EIE scheme compliant software systems
- a user guide (EIE Scheme) that was incorporated into the Inland Revenue's standard documentation.

8.6 Financial EDI

> The fact that you no longer need to write the cheques and post them does not mean you no longer control the payment system.

For many years, the BACS service has helped companies to streamline their payment processes. Like many good ideas, BACS is set to continue to deliver benefits for several years to come. However, BACS is limited in terms of its functional scope and the information it can transfer. Therefore a more comprehensive range of financial messages, based on the international EDIFACT standards, is set to increase the links between businesses and their bankers.

Electronic banking has become increasingly commonplace for companies and individuals, but these services are nearly always specific to one bank. Recognizing the operational benefits from improved financial management, banks have extended the electronic services they provide to their customers. Over and above the traditional BACS service, improved facilities for payment orders, credit advice, direct debits, statements, etc., have been established by several of the major banks over recent years. However, these services have been specific to each bank and a universal solution was clearly needed.

The changes now envisaged will, at last, provide the potential for a single electronic data interchange standard between all banks and their corporate customers. The construction industry, along with representatives from other sectors, has argued for the implementation of such 'common standards', and the tide seems to be turning in our favour.

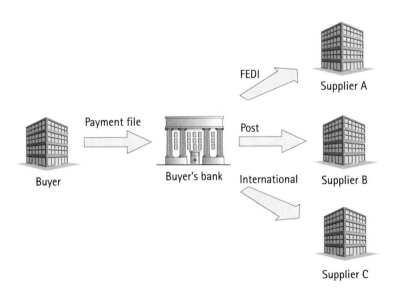

Figure 8.3 FEDI flow - different supplier capabilities

8.6.1 What does financial EDI have to offer?

Using financial EDI (FEDI), banks will be able to receive a single electronic message which, for example, enables them to effect multiple payments and, if required, to send out remittance advice messages. Options to forward the payment and remittance electronically or by paper means that the paying company can move to 100% electronic payments without having to wait for their trading partners to fully implement electronic exchange capabilities (*Figure 8.3*).

Bank charges for FEDI

Although the actual charge will depend on a number of factors, the Royal Bank of Scotland gave an indication of current charges (1997 basis), when the payment instruction is received electronically:

- per cheque raised and processed by the bank, £1.25
- per FEDI payment (paper remittance advice), £0.25 to £0.95 per payment
- per FEDI payment (electronic remittance advice), £0.20 to £0.60 per payment.

Typical accounts payable costs

This will clearly vary from company to company and be influenced by the type of business being transacted. However, the following figures give an view of typical costs incurred *without* FEDI.[20]

Accounts payable	Average	High	Low
Cost per invoice (£/invoice)	3.97	8.62	1.31
Cost per payment (£/payment)	13.45	34.08	5.07
Invoices per payment	3.54	6.57	2.10
No. of invoices per FTE/annum*	7421	16 925	3333
*FTE, full-time equivalent employee			

It was noted at the time when these figures were presented that costs below this level had been achieved within the retail sector where an electronic procurement process was used. The cost benefits from electronic orders, despatch details and invoices were generally agreed to offer a greater cost saving than electronic payments. However, it was stressed that the added benefits from electronic payment systems were well worth having as well.

8.6.2 Things are shaping up!

The UK submitted a proposal for a common framework (based on the international EDIFACT standards) for electronic payment messages to the European FEDI group. This has been accepted in principle, and should increasingly be made available to corporate clients. The framework covers the core exchange messages and will be linked to implementation activities at national level. One further benefit is that it provides a transactional business model for banks and their customers to apply, or adapt, when implementing electronic banking services.

8.6.3 In a nutshell ...

Commercial electronic payment services have been available for some time but have either been limited in scope (e.g. BACS) or been proprietary to individual banks. Further progress to deliver wide-spread access to these benefits clearly requires common exchange standards to be adopted.

UK standards were initially developed during the 1990s by the major high-street banks working with several accounting software providers, but these were not implemented by either group. This was disappointing, especially as it was the banks and software houses that had worked together to create them! However, given the different approach proposed for European (possibly world-wide) standards, this omission has prevented wasted implementation costs. Most of the original UK standards have effectively been made redundant before ever seeing active service. This is a wasted commercial opportunity, though perhaps we should spare a little sympathy for those that were tasked with developing these technical standards!

Now, a European framework for common financial data exchange standards is being agreed. The construction industry has long argued in favour of common standards and welcomes progress in this direction.

8.6.4 What's new?

The adoption of a Europe-wide approach enhances the benefits available to businesses, especially those that operate overseas or with more than one bank. Providing an open framework also puts pressure on banks to provide these services. A common interface, regardless of the bank, or banks, being used by a company, increases interbank competition to retain corporate accounts.

There remains concern about the speed with which implementation of these new standards will be achieved. Clearly much depends on the level of interest being shown by the banks' customers. However, there are signs that major corporations are setting out plans for initial implementations at the earliest possible date. One international company, involved in the message development work, went as far as to say that 'in the foreseeable future they would no longer deal with a bank that did not provide this service'.

8.6.5 Purchase cards

The increasing use of purchase cards within the construction industry has provided many operational benefits. Purchase cards are primarily being used to reduce the administrative costs associated with the processing of local purchase orders by site managers. Several contractors have reported significant benefits from the use of purchase cards. Savings of £60 per local purchase order were reported by Shepherd Construction, but the full impact could be far greater.

Members of the Construction Industry Trading Electronically (CITE) trading group has kept a watchful eye on the increase in the application of purchase cards. The benefits available from the application of purchase cards is set to increase as electronic trading, (including Internet commerce) increases. Recognizing this, CITE enabled its electronic order message to include authorization for payment to be made by providing purchase card details. CITE has also continued to lobby for standardized electronic card statements (including VAT and line item details). Sales outlets are increasingly able to trap VAT details, thus removing the need to obtain a VAT invoice for each transaction.

Shepherd Construction reported that they had over 150 cards in use before the end of 1998 and had already identified notional process savings of £200 000 per annum. Shepherd Construction had also enjoyed knock-on benefits from increased visibility of expenditure. Purchases made by card holders had actually dropped since cards were introduced, and expedient use of materials was thought to be the reason why. Purchases made with these cards incur a fraction of the traditional administrative costs, and cards can be 'blocked', limiting their use to specific categories of outlets. The success of purchase cards has led Shepherd Construction to end the use of local purchase orders for virtually all transactions.

9

Facing the future

> Decision making must be coordinated in a tight and at the same time flexible manner.[21]

9.1 The importance of integrated decision-making

The reason we have all these computers should be to help us make better informed and timely decisions. Therefore we need our applications to help us piece together the jungle of information that informs the decision-makers – which is most of us. There is no shortage of information, computers or even highly functional software, but we are short on integration methods to support effective decision-making.

Computer applications can present information in a highly coordinated and structured manner. For all that, if all they do is echo data we have keyed in, the gain can be very limited. Take a simple

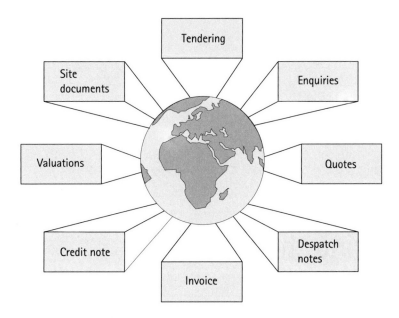

Figure 9.1 Information cycle – data flows through processes, increasing benefits

example: If we key in a list of despatch note numbers into an accounts package and then key in the invoice data to the same package so we can get the computer to see which invoices have a matching despatch note number, we will have achieved an element of process automation. Alternatively, if the despatch note numbers were uploaded directly from site (perhaps by using a real-time radio link to a hand-held scanner) into the accounts package and the invoices were entered directly from an electronic message, the matching process would not only be simplified but could be more detailed.

This example also highlights another link between integration and decision-making. Not all information, or decision-making, occurs in one place. The information available within an enterprise must be available to support the decision-making process, wherever this takes place. Access must be given to the information relevant to each business function, along with a clear understanding of how decisions taken in one area impact on other functions. For this to be possible, all information must be able to be shared across the enterprise (*Figure 9.1*). Whether this is achieved using an Enterprise Resource Planning (ERP) application or by designing effective interfaces between sepa-rate applications is another matter for decision-makers to consider – and for the accountant to value!

However sophisticated your internal applications may be, there is still the need to integrate effectively with external business partners and information sources. Project information from the original design details to the final invoice needs to be able to flow unhindered. This is really very simple to understand and equally simple to prevent. Infor-mation generated at the tender stage should flow directly into the purchasing databases. Data contained within an order should flow back in the invoice, and so on. Preventing this can be as simple as making the field sizes for data elements incompatible or employing a different convention for product definitions within adjacent pro-cesses. Thought must be given, when designing any system, as to how information will flow throughout the entire process within which the particular application resides.

The flexibility needed for decision-making demands a rigidity in interface management. Business applications cannot exploit the information explosion if it is not known how to integrate the informa-tion into the process. It is a bit like delivering a dozen regional reports to a board director, each in electronic form but each written using a different language, knowing that the chief executive has demanded a summary within an hour. Even though all the reports are in electronic form, they can't be read and processed. The same applies to all enter-prise data.

There is a need for a bit of reflection and common sense when designing applications and information systems in the modern busi-ness environment. Information must be presented in a form that most, if not all, can readily integrate with their applications, and applications must support these information formats. A bit less time thinking about powerful individual components and a lot more spent making sure they support an integrated operation would be most welcome. Finally, in case the last comment appears to be pointed at software providers, a significant share of the responsibility for achieving integrated applications lies with the users, who need to specify that this functionality is provided.

9.2 Now look what you've done!

The change in construction practices must be more than a surface treatment:[22]

> For some companies, new technology may simply amount to a significant time saving in keying-in invoices; for others, it will transform the way that they interact with customers, suppliers and project partners.

Even those that have implemented a single electronic exchange document have reported process changes. This may be as simple as recording individual invoice items as compared with bulking groups together, or it might be doing away with invoices and statements and eliminating paper-based drawing exchange.

The truth is, electronic information exchange (EIE) changes nothing – innovators do. We aren't worried about new technology, we are worried about others putting it to better use and gaining a competitive advantage over us. I am sure there are those who wish things just stayed the same, perhaps there are times when we all do. The construction sector has known about EIE for many years. What has changed is that the genie is out of the bottle. Once companies started to apply EIE it was only a matter of time before others would become involved. Each new operation seeks to gain a bit more from the new tools available to them, and so on it goes.

We have to move forward, perhaps recognizing that we have an amount of catching up to do. We only truly recognize change when we look back. At the time we get lulled into a false sense of comfort as everything seems to be happening more slowly than the prophesizers would have us believe. But, when we look back over the last ten years we see changes in our industry many said would never happen.

International companies now own UK-based contractors, professional clients are increasingly managing significant parts of their projects and Internet access is a basic business requirement. There was no big bang, no vote in the Commons and no date on which anyone can say these changes took place – they just gradually came to be. Lots of little decisions finally create a critical mass, a phenomenon I can only define as 'when most people agree something has come to be ... if only over a cup of coffee'. To me the issue is more about inevitability, a state that comes before achieving the critical mass. Companies that spot the inevitable should have the most time to adapt effectively to change and a chance to achieve a differential over their competitors, if only until the rest catch up.

I have no doubt we have reached the inevitable point when force feeding data to computers on bits of paper can no longer be considered a viable business process. The impact of the Internet and Government drives to increase our adoption of electronic commerce will simply not allow this subject to go away.

9.3 Will things ever be the same again?

I doubt very much that you need me to answer this question, but I would like to provide a few indicators as to where change is likely to occur. My intention is not to set out a view of the future, but rather to support and encourage a belief that EIE can be used to transform processes (see Section 9.4). Simply replacing paper with data will not be enough for most businesses to remain competitive.

As business managers we can be worried by the possibility of endless change and our ability to keep up with the pace. In reality, things seldom move that fast, even with the Internet. What makes things seem so fast is that we don't change gradually ourselves. Most businesses monitor what is going on and then put on a spurt to catch up. Others might manage a steady progression, even keeping to the forefront (well someone has to be at the front!). Just a few have little idea about the impact of change until they are suddenly forced into action.

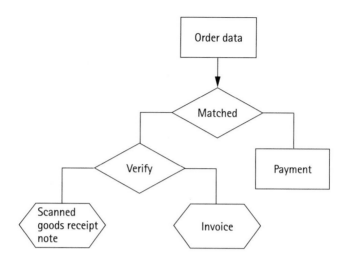

Figure 9.2 From delivery to payment – approach 1

I would encourage managers to seek the 'little and often' approach to change, especially with EIE. With new headline-grabbing Internet developments filling the press month on month it is hard not to feel out of touch. In reality, most EIE developments are nothing like as exciting or difficult as indicated by the hype. Keeping close to the front gives us a better view and a clearer ability to separate the wheat from the chaff. So, as has ever been the case, things will never be the same again – but change is our opportunity to do things better, our opportunity to improve our performance against that of our competitors.

9.4 Some examples of process change opportunities

In this section I model some processes, showing how they could be operated using the operational characteristics of EIE. These are not ultimate solutions, rather several first steps that could be taken in the ongoing journey towards integrated systems. It is important to note that there is not a single correct solution, and that electronic exchange documents can be used within completely different business models. To emphasize the flexibility of common standards, the first two models look at the same process.

9.4.1 Goods receipt, with electronic invoices

In this model (*Figure 9.2*), the delivery note number is recorded at site by scanning a bar code on the delivery note. Variations, such as incorrect delivery quantity, could also be recorded using the hand-held scanner, and the combined records uploaded the accounts/procurement system. On receipt of the electronic invoice, a verification check could automatically confirm whether the goods had been received. Once past this stage, invoices are then matched against order data before be cleared for payment.

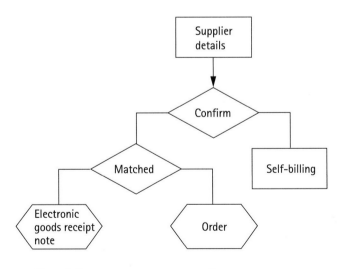

Figure 9.3 From delivery to payment – approach 2

9.4.2 Goods receipt, with electronic despatch information exchange

In this case (*Figure 9.3*) the delivery information is supplied electronically. The same scanning option can be used on site. The next stage is to match the delivery information to the order details (it would be recommended that an electronic order has been exchanged between the purchaser and supplier) to confirm that the goods received had been ordered. A further check confirms the payment status of the supplier and then, where applicable, a self-billing invoice can be raised to authorize payment to the supplier.

9.4.3 Paperless tenders

The contracts, custom and practice, and caution that surrounds the process of requesting and submitting bids for a construction project has vexed those involved for years. That said, breaking the habit has proved more than a little challenging. Nonetheless, there are those who are cautiously drawing up plans to break with tradition. The following is one such idea.

Where a contract requires the submission of tenders, the client or their consultant could compile the drawings, preliminary details and the bill of quantities in electronic format. Rather than printing sets for each of the half-dozen or so bidding contractors, a single set of electronic document could be uploaded to a secure Web site. A simple e-mail is then sent to each bidding contractor confirming that the documents are ready to download and giving them their unique password.

The e-mail could require an auto-acknowledgement and the time at which each contractor downloads the files can be recorded. The bids can be returned in the same manner and, where simultaneous opening is required, a third-party controlled site could be used. Although legislation supporting the use of digital signatures and certificates should negate the need for a contractual paper copy, those involved in this process would hardly begrudge one printout of the winning bid, as this would be a fraction of the traditional reams involved.

9.4.4 Project information exchange

From architects' instructions to day works, certificates and transmittal notes, construction managers and all parties to the project generate large quantities of formal documents. What is more, each document can be critical to the process. Handwritten, word-processed documents, faxes and e-mails soon start to accumulate on desks and in filing cabinets.

The model here is simple: each project partner uses a computer-based project/information system of their choosing, provided each can exchange documents according to a common exchange standard. Messages can be exchanged across the Internet or perhaps via a project Web site. Each partner receives their messages with the minimum of delay. More importantly, all documents look the same to each recipient, improving confidence in their correct interpretation. Each partner (and a central project database) will have an archive of documents sent and received which should speed up query resolution and, hopefully, prevent some problems from ever arising. At the end of the contract, the full set of exchanged documents could be copied to a CD and retained as a permanent record.

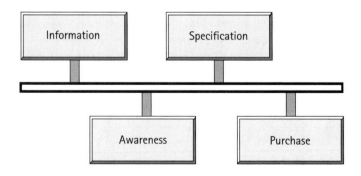

Figure 9.4 Product selection – how it often is

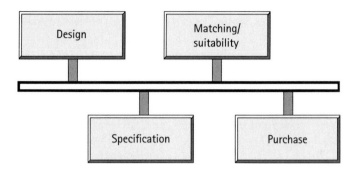

Figure 9.5 Product selection – how it increasingly might be

9.4.5 Product selection

Traditionally, designers, specifiers and buyers have been bombarded with information about products they could use to meet a certain requirement. Very often the information arrives when there is no current need for the item or, worse still, when the item is required it can't be found in the library (or pile in the corner) (*Figure 9.4*). Thus, information is received and hopefully retained. When a particular project need arises, awareness of the most appropriate item will be the driver defining what is specified and purchased.

When product information becomes more widely available in electronic form (standardized!), it then becomes possible to collect much larger quantities of data. It is also possible to receive the information without viewing it all or deciding where it should be archived. Now, when a design generates a specification for a particular item, the product database can be searched for suitable options (*Figure 9.5*). Information presented could include pictures, tables, descriptions, latest pricing offers, etc. The person responsible can then select the most appropriate option. Product databases could be constantly updated, either by purchasing packaged information, receiving update files from key manufacturers/suppliers, by downloading Web site files or by a combination of all three. New products will more readily find themselves identified as a viable option and overall product selection should more closely meet the clients' demands.

10

Closing remarks

I doubt that it will be long before we not only see, but take for granted, the role that electronic information exchange (EIE) plays in enabling business managers to achieve their commercial goals. I also expect that this impact will have more to do with the innovators than with the innovation. The benefits from linking applications electronically are desirable, achievable and increasingly essential to a modern business. There is no shortage of technology, but there has been a shortage of application.

Each year, the latest communication technologies will be set before us, each offering new ways to integrate business systems. However, the basic approach to implementation will change little, if at all, from that set out in this book. Our internal applications must support our operations, and our operations must be integrated with those of our trading partners. The objective will remain that we maximise quality and client benefits at lowest cost.

Construction businesses cannot remain competitive using traditional communication methods. Neither is it acceptable to keep watching technological advances without understanding the clear impact they will have on our industry. The writing is more than 'on the wall' and companies must determine how to remain competitive in a changing commercial world.

The increased use of computer applications has provided the opportunity to streamline and integrate operations across all process elements. The threat is that we believe old process models, based on discrete businesses, can co-exist with those driven by whole-process benefits and integrated systems. Companies that do not plan, at strategic decision level, to adopt or exploit electronic exchange risk becoming uncompetitive or too far off the pace to afford to catch up. EIE will cease to be a limiting factor, being replaced in this role by our ability to exploit its potential to transform business processes. Adopting EIE, which currently sounds innovative, will eventually no longer be sufficient to remain fully competitive.

The good news is that the construction sector may leapfrog other industries as it implements EIE. Given the low penetration of such technologies during the 1980s and 1990s, the explosion in electronic business, stimulated by the Internet, can be embraced without replacing existing services. New standards, such as XML, can be adopted as the primary data language, while other industries continue to use older standards, or require costly migration paths forward.

One way or another, we will link our computer applications together. We should strive to adopt a single data language and always to remain focused on business benefits. Collecting new exchange services, like Scout or Guide badges, makes little sense as does 'doing nothing' while falling further and further behind the pace.

The answer lies with informed decision-makers delivering incremental change. Lesson one in identifying opportunities for change is to look around your business and challenge each data entry activity as to whether this is the best way to get information into the application. Step two is to challenge the very process that surrounds each activity.

My final request is that we don't overcomplicate matters. In a subject littered with jargon and techno-babble it is easy to be put off or, worse still, led to believe this subject is beyond our understanding.

Moving information directly from one computer to another is merely the simple and logical consequence of using computers. Computers are intrinsically linked to the daily contributions we each make in the world of work. Therefore, they too must be part of effective business communications – part of the team.

Appendix 1. Information about eCentre^{uk}

The following information draws largely, mostly verbatim, upon a submission document by eCentre^{uk} and its members to the Trade and Industry Committee inquiry on electronic commerce which was produced in 1999.[23]

What is eCentre^{UK}?

eCentre^{UK} was formed by the merger of the Article Number Association (ANA) with the Electronic Commerce Association (ECA) on 1 October 1998. eCentre^{UK} seeks to add value to its members by being the pre-eminent, most trusted source of the best standards for business data and the best practices for electronic commerce. eCentre^{UK} is a non-profit-making body incorporated as a company limited by guarantee, and is a member of EAN International (The international Article Numbering organization), which is represented in 90 countries worldwide. The association provides help and advice on electronic commerce to UK organizations and provides a comprehensive suite of services to its members to help them to adopt best practice in doing business electronically across the extended enterprise.

Summary of main points

Recognizing that the UK must maintain and increase its competitiveness through using best practice in electronic commerce as widely as possible, and noting the Government's aim to make the UK 'world leaders by the end of this parliament', we believe that the UK must to do the following:

- Trust and confidence in electronic commerce must be instilled by enacting a crisp, clear, business-supportive bill on secure electronic commerce during this session of Parliament.
- An increase in UK competitiveness will be supported by the maximum use of electronic commerce by business.
- Awareness and training activity needs to focus on small to medium sized enterprises (SMEs). It needs to be relevant, provided locally, backed by a centre of expertise and then supported by the availability of good off-the-shelf software packages.
- Government needs to make maximum use of electronic commerce to improve efficiency and to become an exemplar for all.
- We must all act quickly if the UK is to maintain, and develop, its potentially strong position over electronic commerce.
- Organizations like eCentre[UK] need to receive project-related funding from the Department of Trade and Industry (DTI) (in the way that the US Government supported CommerceNet) if the UK is to become a world leader in electronic commerce in its own right.

Electronic commerce

In the quest to maintain market position or gain competitive advantage by streamlining operations, reducing costs and improving customer service, businesses are increasingly turning to electronic commerce. Electronic commerce enables organizations of all sizes and in all market sectors to improve their competitiveness. It cuts across geographic boundaries and time zones to save time and costs, to open up new market opportunities and to enable even the smallest of companies to compete on a global stage. Electronic commerce spans established processes such as bar-code scanning and electronic data interchange (EDI) as well as newer arrivals, such as e-mail, the Internet, the World Wide Web and mobile electronic commerce. At the ECA, one of the antecedents of eCentre^{UK}, we have taken a broad definition and, put simply, electronic commerce can be defined as:

> doing business electronically ... across the extended enterprise.

At a more detailed level the definition reads:

> Electronic commerce covers any form of business or administrative transaction or information exchange that is executed using any information and communications technology (ICT).

This embraces the three main areas of activity, namely: business to business; business to consumer; and Government to nation (that includes both businesses and the citizen).

The Internet needs no introduction, but its use as a business medium is still in its early stages. Estimates vary widely, but analysts all agree that the next few years will see an explosion in electronic commerce, fuelled in large part by the Internet. It provides a medium that is as easily useable by individuals as by organizations in both the public and private sector, opening up hitherto impossible or innovative possibilities, providing instant access to products and services worldwide and posing challenges to business and Government alike.

Trading electronically

Internet technology may be new and attracting media and public attention, but business to business trading by electronic means has been heavily in use and actively developed for nearly twenty-five

years. The Article Number Association (ANA), the other anteced-
ent of eCentre^{UK}, was actively involved from the start of article
numbering and bar coding by helping to create the EAN International open standard language. This has had a positive impact on all
sectors of business and administration in all countries.

To improve further the accuracy and efficiency gains achieved, it
quickly developed and introduced the first truly electronic trade message standards, which enabled a company's computers to speak
directly to other companies' computers without human intervention.
Generically known as electronic data interchange (EDI), the ANA
based its own system on a United Nations protocol and called it
TRADACOMS. To enable companies to gain maximum advantage
from TRADACOMS by being able to trade electronically with many
other partners, the ANA devised, encouraged and licensed the operator of the first value added network (VAN), a private and primitive
form of 'Internet', which it called TRADANET. Household names,
such as Sainsbury, Tesco, Nestle and Procter & Gamble, aggressive
competitors in the public eye, were among the earliest to appreciate
the value of standard numbers used in bar codes and EDI. They all
joined the ANA at the beginning in 1976 and have continued to take
active roles in the development of numbering, bar coding and EDI.
These member companies and many others from a range of diverse
industrial and business sectors that have been involved from the earliest days of EAN numbering, bar coding and EDI are now at the
forefront of electronic commerce using the latest Internet
technologies.

The Government's proposals for legislation on secure electronic commerce, announced in the Queen's Speech

Users of electronic commerce need to have trust and confidence in
doing business electronically and at present they lack that confidence
which the planned Bill would be an important part of building. We
believe that eCentre^{UK} has a significant, continuing role to play in

helping the DTI develop the optimum legislation, especially in developing codes of practice. We need a crisp, clear bill as soon as possible.

Electronic payment systems

Electronic commerce represents an opportunity for a rapid move by businesses to electronic payment, especially in SMEs. In order for the UK to unlock this potential the main issues are:

- integration of electronic commerce facilities in standard (off-the-shelf) accounting/purchasing software
- interoperability between message standards developed for EDI and the newer electronic commerce technologies such as XML and XML/EDI
- ensuring that UK developments are compatible with internationally agreed standards
- general implementation of the purchase card.

An area of significant potential is the combination of the digital certification trust services with payment systems. DTI can provide a lead to UK business by encouraging UK Government procurement areas to be early adopters of these trust services/payment methods in their forthcoming implementation of electronic commerce procurement.

Electronic Government

Together with the other members of the Alliance for Electronic Business, we believe that Government has a key role to play as a model user of electronic commerce. Since all businesses and citizens deal with Government there is a strong opportunity to lead by example through implementing best practice in electronic commerce.

The opportunities for cost savings and greatly improved efficiency are considerable, especially in procurement. We welcome the Government's initiative to encourage its departments to embrace electronic purchasing. Some good work has been done throughout

Government in the purchasing arena to optimize efficiencies, and there is now a golden opportunity for the UK to lead the world in this area.

EAN has had an International Electronic Catalogue Project Team working on the definition of a Product Catalogue based on the international product numbering standards. We believe that it is important for Government to adopt these standards in its development of open catalogues for procurement.

Automatic data capture needs to be used to a much greater extent in Government procurement and asset trading.

eCentre^{UK} believes that Government has a great opportunity to encourage UK (and European) software companies by obtaining the necessary software solutions from them, rather than from the USA.

Improving the awareness and understanding of electronic commerce in UK business (especially helping SMEs)

Improved awareness and understanding of electronic commerce continues to be the key issue for all sizes of business and all regions of the UK. We need to train the trainers to develop local expertise on a nationwide basis. UK competitiveness is held back because of the lack of readily available knowledge amongst the business advisors.

Many UK companies, especially SMEs, are still complacent about the threats to their business if they do not take up the opportunities offered by electronic commerce. The majority of our members are SMEs, and we know that working with and helping them requires tailored resources.

eCentre^{UK} seeks to work closely with the DTI in developing best practice guidelines and awareness, in electronic commerce. We believe very strongly that the Business Links, Chambers of Commerce, Technology Webs and Local Support Centres need stronger focus and drive from the centre. At present there are many spokes without a clear hub providing best practice and training.

It is very important to ensure that local advisors have a strong understanding of the business issues of electronic commerce, as well as the technical ones. eCentre^UK looks forward to further work with the DTI, and its Information Society Initiative, to publicize best practice case studies, to extend its current involvement in the annual Awards for Innovation in Electronic Commerce and to develop further awareness materials and local seminars.

We also believe that the E-commerce Resource Centre on the Internet, proposed in the DTI's recent White Paper on Competitiveness (see Digital Economy, paragraph 3.18), is a natural extension of the current facilities offered by eCentre^UK, and we would welcome the opportunity to develop that with the DTI.

Business on the Internet – open business standards

The ready availability of Internet-based technology is dramatically changing the opportunities and facilities available to business. Large businesses, that have been trading electronically for some time, are having to review these new opportunities in their business to business transactions, and also have the prospect of dealing electronically directly with the consumer. The SMEs are faced with the same set of new opportunities, but often without the background in electronic trading. An important part of these communications in the Internet environment is the use of business information standards. eCentre^UK is active in these developments, to ensure a level playing field for all users of electronic commerce and would welcome development support from the DTI.

Data capture technologies

There is a spectrum of data carriers – bar codes (linear and two-dimensional), radiofrequency tags, smart cards, EDI, the Internet – all of which in different but complementary ways should contribute to and enable new ways of managing business–business, business–customer and Government–citizen relationships. Real understanding and encouragement for these can generate new service industries.

Strategic policy and international interactions

It is important that the UK 'punches its weight' in the international arenas where global strategy is being set (e.g. the World Trade Organization, the Organization for Economic and Co-operation and Development (OECD), G8, the International Organization for Standardization and the United Nations), so that the opportunities for UK competitiveness in a global setting are maximized.

The DTI should lead the field in such coordination by establishing a public–private sector partnership that enables the key UK influences in electronic commerce to determine a national and international framework for electronic commerce. We therefore reiterate our previous proposal to the DTI for the formation of a National Electronic Commerce Committee, driven by private and public sector users. It should consist of senior private and public sector figures working together to set a UK strategy for electronic commerce and to guide the 'e-Envoy' in his or her work.

The role of the DTI as a focal point for electronic commerce in the UK

Aspects of electronic commerce cut across many parts of the DTI and across many parts of other Government departments – indeed they impinge on most departments and their work. The DTI needs to enhance this focusing role, both internally and externally. Again, the appointment of the e-Envoy and formation of a National Electronic Commerce Committee (led by users from private and public sector) is key to this.

The development of an efficient, totally integrated supply chain, in both the private and public sector

The reality of economic activity is that there is a vast Web of interactions between organizations of all kinds, both world-wide and with individual consumers of goods and services. In this context it is necessary to have an international standard language that enables the relevant data to be exchanged seamlessly and used unambiguously in all organizations' systems.

In their work with European Informatics Market (EURIM), eCentre^{UK} recommended the application of more resources and effort to link best business practice, electronic commerce, EDI and IT applications, to improve UK value chain communications and operations, especially for SMAs. This will also benefit the 'better Government' initiative.

Government is part of this extended, global electronic value chain. It must integrate its procedures with those of the private sector, by working together with others. It must adopt electronic commerce in its own processes, both to improve the effectiveness and efficiency of Government and to be an exemplar to the private sector.

International trade

To ensure harmonization of trade procedures and electronic commerce we would encourage greater links between the Simpler Trade Procedures Board (SITPRO) and eCentre^{UK}, because no single organization can handle this alone. We strongly support SITPRO's ElecTra project, which is developing simplified, standard electronic forms to simplify export procedures. UK competitiveness requires further simplification and streamlining of trade procedures, especially customs procedures.

Conclusion

Development of electronic commerce is moving very rapidly.

We have noticed and welcomed the more active role that the DTI has been taking of late to develop UK competitiveness through electronic commerce. This needs to continue and be accelerated. Electronic commerce is growing apace and the UK needs to move rapidly if it really is going to develop its current strong position and be a world leader. eCentre^{UK}, together with the other members of the Alliance for Electronic Business (the other members are the Confederation of British Industry and the Computer Software and Services Association) aims to have a central role in that process and to seek strong support from the DTI.

Appendix 2. HM Customs and Excise electronic invoice requirements

EDI Annexe

Requirements imposed by the Commissioners of Customs and Excise under paragraph 3(2) of Schedule 7 to the Value Added Tax Act 1983

A   Issue of tax invoices by direct transmission

1. You first make a trial run of the computer system to be used for the production and processing of invoices by means of direct transmission, notify the Commissioners of the time when you propose to hold the trial run and give the Commissioners the opportunity to observe the trial run and to inspect the results thereof.

2. You must give the Commissioners one month's notice of any significant alteration in the system which is in operation.

3. For each computer file of documents which are tax invoices by virtue of paragraph 3 of Schedule 7 to the Value Added Tax Act 1983, or which are produced as a result of the transmission by electronic means of the requisite particulars and treated as the provision of tax invoices by virtue of that section, and for every copy thereof, you must compile a summary control document which shall be handwritten, typewritten or printed; the summary control document shall identify the computer file to which it relates and shall state:

    (a) the total number and description of each type of document on that file;

    (b) for each rate of tax the total tax exclusive value of supplies mentioned in that file;

    (c) the total tax charges at each rate on the supplies mentioned in that file;
    and

    (d) the total value of exempt supplies mentioned in that file.

    The summary control document for a copy of a file shall state clearly that the file is a copy of another file. You shall preserve a copy of each summary control document with your records and shall provide a copy to the receiver of the supplies. Any notification of disagreement sent by the receiver of the supplies must be resolved by you.

4. The information recorded on each computer file as mentioned in paragraph 3 above shall include a unique version number or some other unique identification, and the totals set out at 3(a) to (d) above for all supplies mentioned in the file.

5. You shall, if the Commissioners so require, provide or arrange for the provision of a certificate in accordance with section 5(4) of the Civil Evidence Act 1968.

6. Providing all the above requirements are fully complied with, the requirements of Regulation 13(1) of the Value Added Tax (General) Regulations 1985 will be relaxed to following extent:-

(a) your name, address and VAT registration number; and

(b) the name and address of the person to whom the goods or services are supplied

may be recorded once per computer file rather than once per invoice.

7. I would also like to take this opportunity of advising you of certain other requirements/conditions concerning the operation of your new system which are governed by other sections of VAT legislation. You must:

(a) preserve your copy of each control document provided together with any notification of disagreement document provided to them and any associated file or data for a period of 6 years from the provision of the documents or the creation of the file or data or any shorter period as may be approved in writing by the local VAT office (paragraph 7 of Schedule 7 to the Value Added Tax Act 1983);

(b) as required by the Commissioners furnish them with particulars in legible form on paper of any supplies made (paragraph 8 of Schedule 7 to the Value Added Tax Act 1983); and

(c) allow the Commissioners to inspect and check the operation of any computer which is or has been used in connection with the production of tax invoices or the transmission of the requisite particulars of tax invoices (Finance Act 1985, Section 10).

Requirements (general)

B Receipt invoices by direct transmission

Requirements imposed by the Commissioners of Customs and Excise under paragraph 3(2) of Schedule 7 to the Value Added Tax Act 1983.

1. You must first make a trial run of the computer system to be used for the receipt and processing of invoices by means of direct transmission, notify the Commissioners of the time when you propose to hold the trial run and give the Commissioners the opportunity to observe the trial run and to inspect the results thereof.

2. You must give the Commissioners one month's notice of any significant alteration in the system which is in operation.

3. For each computer file of documents which are tax invoices by virtue of paragraph 3 of Schedule 7 to the Value Added Tax Act 1983, or which are produced as a result of the transmission by electronic means of the requisite particulars and treated as the provision of tax invoices by virtue of that section, and for every copy thereof, you must obtain from the supplier of the file a summary control document, which shall be handwritten, typewritten or printed; the summary control document shall identify the computer file to which it relates, and shall state:

    (a) the total number and description of each type of document on that file;

    (b) for each rate of tax the total tax exclusive value of supplies mentioned in that file;

    (c) the total tax charged at each rate on supplies mentioned in that file; and

    (d) the total value of exempt supplies mentioned in that file.

    The summary control document for a copy of a file shall state clearly that the file is a copy of another file. You shall preserve the summary control document with your records.

4. For each computer file of documents which are invoices by virtue of paragraph 3 of Schedule 7 to the Value Added Tax Act 1983 and for every copy thereof, you shall recalculate the totals set out at 3 (a) to (d) above for all supplies mentioned in the file. If there is any disagreement you shall compile a notification document which shall be handwritten, typewritten or printed in respect of any disagreement; you shall preserve a copy of this

document with your records and shall provide another copy to the supplier of the file.

5. The information recorded on each computer file as mentioned in paragraphs 3 and 4 above shall include a unique version number or some other identification, and the totals set out at 3(a) to (d) above.

6. Any system which reads such computer files as are mentioned in paragraphs 3, 4 and 5 shall incorporate an inhibit which will prevent the same file from being input more than once for any given function.

7. You shall, if the Commissioners so require, provide or arrange for the provision of a certificate in accordance with section 5(4) of the Civil Evidence Act 1968.

8. I would also like to take this opportunity of advising you of certain other requirements/conditions concerning the operation of your new system which are governed by other sections of the VAT legislation. You must:

    (a) preserve each control document together with a copy of any notification of disagreement document issued by you and any associated file or data for a period of six years from the provision of the documents or the creation of the file or data or any shorter period as may be approved in writing by a local VAT office (paragraph 7 of Schedule 7 to the Value Added Tax Act 1983);

    (b) as required by the Commissioners furnish them with particulars in legible form on paper of any supplies received (paragraph 8 of Schedule 7 to the Value Added Tax Act 1983); and

    (c) allow the Commissioners to inspect and check the operation of any computer used in connection with the receipt of tax invoices or the transmission of the requisite particulars of tax invoices (Finance Act 1985, Section 10).

Appendix 3. Introductory section from the Guidelines for using XML for Electronic Data Interchange

Source: The SGML Centre, Editor Martin Bryan, Version 0.05.

Purpose & Goal of the XML/EDI Guidelines

Put simply, the goal of XML/EDI is to deliver unambiguous and durable business transactions via electronic means. Associated with this is a goal to establish a standard for commercial electronic data interchange that is open and accessible to all, and which delivers a broad spectrum of capabilities suitable to meet the full breadth of business needs.

To achieve this requires the use of a methodology that it is not only extensible enough to meet future requirements but also adaptable enough to incorporate new technologies and requirements as they emerge. To ensure broad adoption the technology selected needs to be widely and freely available. The Extensible Mark-up Language (XML) developed by the World Wide Web Consortium (W3C) provides such a freely available, widely transportable, methodology for well-controlled data interchange.

XML was designed principally for the exchange of information in the form of computer displayable "documents". Not all commercial data is interchanged in a displayable format. In particular data designed for electronic data interchange typically needs to be processed before it can be displayed. For this to be possible the data must be mapped, using some form of template, to a set of processing rules. These XML/EDI guidelines provide a standardized way in which such rules templates can be added to interchanged data.

These XML/EDI guidelines begin by formally defining the terms used in the text. This is followed by an impact statement that makes predictions from various viewpoints. The guidelines then give a background on the tools and standards which XML/EDI is built.

Note: These guidelines form the basis for development work on XML/EDI, They form an precursor to a formal "Specification of an EDI Application for XML". As a document designed to be a lighting rod for ideas, this working document has been, and will continue to be, released in draft form. Comments on this draft should be sent to the XML/EDI working group at xml-edi@riv.be.

Definitions for XML/EDI

Electronic commerce has been defined in the European Workshop on Open System's Technical Guide on Electronic Commerce (EWOS ETG 066) as 'Electronic exchange of data to support business transactions, i.e. the exchange of value through the delivery of a product from a seller to a buyer'. As such it encompasses much more than what has been possible using traditional methods of Electronic Data Interchange (EDI) such as EDIFACT. Electronic commerce is defined by EWOS as covering activities such as marketing, contract exchange, logistics support, settlement and interaction with administrative bodies (e.g. tax and custom data interchange). Electronic commerce covers all industrial and service operations, including services such as insurance, healthcare, travel and interactive home shopping.

Many people use the term EDI to refer to the set of messages developed for business-to-business communication as part of the United Nations Standard Messages Directory for Electronic Data interchange for Administration, Commerce and Transport (EDIFACT). EDIFACT messages are transmitted in compressed form, using predefined field identifiers, which must occur in a predefined sequence. While EDI is, strictly speaking, wider in scope than EDIFACT, for the purposes of these guidelines EDI will be used in this restricted sense when not otherwise qualified.

The basic unit of information in an EDI message is the data element. For an EDI invoice, each item being invoiced would be represented by a data element. Data elements can be grouped into compound data elements, and data elements and/or compound data elements may be grouped into data segments. Data segments can be grouped into loops and loops and/or data segments form business documents.

The EDIFACT standards define whether data segments are mandatory, optional, or conditional, and indicate whether, how many times, and in what order a particular data segment can be repeated. For each EDI message, a field definition table exists. For each data segment, the field definition table includes a key field identifier string to indicate the data elements to be included in the data segment, the sequence of the elements, whether each element is mandatory, optional, or conditional, and the form of each element in terms of the number of characters and whether the characters are numeric or alphabetic. Similarly, field definition tables include data element identifier strings to describe individual data elements. Element identifier strings define an element's name, a reference designator, a data dictionary reference number specifying the location in a data dictionary where information on the data element can be found, a requirement designator (either mandatory, optional, or conditional), a type (such as numeric, decimal, or alphanumeric), and a length (minimum and maximum number of characters). A data element dictionary gives the content and meaning for each data element

Originally, EDI translation software was developed to support a variety of private system formats. Most often, the sender and receiver were required to contract in advance for a tailored software program that would be dedicated to mapping between their two types of datasets. Each time a new sender or receiver was added to the client list, a new translation program would be needed by the new party to format their data to conform to the standards in use by the participants. Of course, this becomes expensive. Such static systems do not easily allow synchronization of business transactions in distributed business processes that involve global rules, but with participants and actions that are not predetermined. To solve these issues it is desirable to develop automated tools and techniques that are easy to use and allow decomposition of transactions in actions to be performed locally and mapping of local actions onto efficient protocol exchanges.

Appendix 5. The International Alliance for Interoperability (IAI)

Introduction

Twelve companies involved in the AEC/FM Industry in the USA started the IAI. They wanted to be able to work with one another's information without being concerned about the software used. They created a series of prototype software applications which were demonstrated at the A/E/C Systems '95 show in Atlanta, Georgia. These prototypes proved that interoperability was not just a dream: it could be made into a reality.

With this successful public demonstration, the original twelve companies opened up participation in this effort in September 1995 to AEC/FM companies world-wide. Interest spread rapidly, with a Chapter being established in Germany in December 1995 and in the

UK in January 1996. There are now nine Chapters with representation from 20 countries and 650 member organizations worldwide.

IAI's vision, mission and values

(1) IAI's vision is 'to enable software interoperability in the AEC/FM industry'.
(2) To achieve this vision, it has defined its mission as being 'to provide a universal basis for process improvement and information sharing in the construction and facilities management industries'.
(3) The values of the IAI are stated as follows:
   - not-for-profit industry organization
   - membership open to any company working in the AEC/FM industry
   - action oriented: alliance rather than association
   - consensus-based decision-making
   - incremental delivery rather than prolonged study
   - global solution
   - AEC/FM industry professionals working with software professionals to define standard specification
   - specification to be open for implementation and use by all software vendors
   - design for specification to be extensible
   - specification will evolve over time.

IAI organization and operation

Each Chapter is a separate organization and is established according to local custom. In the UK, the Chapter is a company limited by guarantee.

The IAI membership includes architects, engineers, contractors, building owners and managers, building product manufacturers, software vendors, information providers, government agencies, research laboratories and universities. The individuals representing these companies have skills which fall into two general categories:

- domain experts are individuals involved with the daily practice of their expertise in the building industry, such as architects, engineers, contractors and facility managers
- technical experts are individuals with a background in research, software design and engineering and typically have some experience in the AEC/FM industry.

Each Chapter has established 'domain committees' suited to their representative members. Each domain committee is interested in a particular discipline, such as architecture or building services, or a process, such as construction or facilities management. Domain committee members have experience in the domain's specialization. A domain expert chairs the committee. A specialist assists the chair in the development of software specifications (or models). Each committee typically includes other domain specialists and technical experts.

A domain committee within a Chapter joins with similar domains elsewhere in projects to develop a specification or model of the information content of a business process of interest and value to them.

Groups

(1) Technical work is carried out in four specialist groups. Each Group has a specific set of tasks. Tasks are fulfilled by 'capability teams' within the Groups and it is a responsibility of the Group Leader to locate and ensure the availability of resources within the capability teams.

(2) The Implementation Support Group (ISG) takes on the role of the previous Implementation Committee but with more targeted tasks in ensuring the quality and implementability of the IFC model. For these purposes, it will work closely with the Model Support Group (MSG) to achieve the following:

- quality assurance of the IFC model to ensure that it can be implemented
- certification
- cooperation with MSG
- prototype development
- software demonstrations.

(3) The Model Support Group (MSG) takes on a number of roles particularly in respect of the integration of the IFC model and its documentation. This group consists of modelling specialists selected for their proven skills. An additional task of this group is to develop an Integrated Reference Process Model that is expected to grow in importance to IAI members as a tool to assist business improvement through the use of object technology. Its work covers the following:

- IFC technical architecture
- integration of data model
- integration of process model
- resolution of model issues
- documentation support
- hotline.

(4) The User Support Group (USG) takes on roles which affect the development of projects and the dissemination of information concerning IFCs on a wider scale. It provides model support to projects to assist them in bringing their models to the highest possible quality for integration within IFC. The USG also coordinates IFC demonstration projects and helps those who wish to develop a demonstration project. Its work may be summed up as:

- IFC development methodology
- information to users
- technical marketing
- project model support
- development and coordination of demonstration projects.

(5) The Technical Advisory Group (TAG) takes on the role of providing guidance on the future technologies that need to be

considered in IFC development. It also facilitates review of the IFC model by specialists (who need not be members of the IAI), part of the IAI policy to ensure the highest possible quality of the IFC Object Model. A further task is to progress academic development and use of IFCs within colleges and universities and to extend this to research and development projects. Finally, TAG coordinates the development of the IFC Roadmap to plan what is needed in the future. This will take input from the other groups and from the broader membership of the IAI. To sum up, its work is:

- external review of models
- liaison with other bodies
- academic development
- coordination of roadmap development.

Appendix 4. The XCAT project (linking the EDIFACT catalogue message with XML)

Source: Project documentation available from XCAT Web sites (e.g. www.fl.dk).

Project description

With the introduction of XML/EDI, the use of traditional EDI is faced with a new challenge: how do we take advantage of a technology that potentially brings EDI into any Web browser anywhere in the world?

Soon it will be possible to offer EDI solutions to (industry) segments that traditionally reject EDI due to high costs and complexity.

It is, however, important to preserve the knowledge that is represented in more than 200 EDIFACT messages. Implementing the existing messages into XML/EDI achieves this.

The XML/EDI framework opens the door to a new paradigm for processing documents and completing transactions. Using standards to access components of XML documents and adding style information to XML documents, XML/EDI documents and included objects can be exchanged, viewed, searched, catalogued, and routed ('pushed'). The XML/EDI framework provides all the fundamental building blocks of electronic commerce (e-commerce).

XML/EDI has the potential to change the way organizations manage and transfer their business information. While Internet XML is only just taking off, by 1999 XML/EDI has the potential of becoming one of the dominant forces in e-commerce

1. Purpose of the project

Although XML/EDI has a large potential as a means to bridge the gap between Web and EDI-based commerce, very few practical examples exist in Denmark as well as internationally. Thus the current professional evaluation of XML/EDI is based on concepts rather than experience.

To overcome this, the XCAT project presented here converts an EDIFACT message (PRICAT) to XML and vice versa. By doing this, the consortium has gained hands-on experience with the technology.

2. Expected results

The project was expected to produce the following results/ deliverables:

- A DTD for PRICAT. Document type definitions (DTDs) formally define the
- relationships of the attributes that form a particular class of EDI messages.

- An XSL for PRICAT. The style sheet (XSL) defines the presentation of the data contained in the XML document.
- A demo on the Internet.

It was decided not to produce an XSL, as the international work of defining the structures is still in progress.

3. The actual result

The actual result of the XCAT project is first of all a demonstration illustrating hail XML can be used for EDI transactions – a hands-on demo is available on the Web at www.edi.dk, www.fl.dk/xcat, www.systematic.dk/xcat or www.uniware.dk/xcat.

Furthermore, the project has resulted in the development of a DTD for the EDIFACT PRICAT message. Due to the projects tight time schedule, a full documentation of this DTD is not available.

Unfortunately it was not technically possible to develop an XSL-based display for the XML PRICAT message as it was originally intended. The reason is that at the time of the development, XSL was not supported by standard browsers.

4. Members of the consortium

- The Danish EDI-Council (www.edi.dk).
- Fischer & Lorenz A/S (www.fl.dk).
- Systematic Software Engineering A/S (www.systematic.dk).
- UNIWARE danmark A/S (www.uniware.dk).

5. Lessons learned

The purpose of this chapter is to pass on the consortium's practical experiences of what to do and what not to do when creating an EDIFACT to XML converter.

5.1. First lesson learned: it actually works!

Needs no further explanation.

5.2. Second lesson learned: what structure should be used?

In the demo setting we chose to lean heavily on the EDIFACT structure to make sure that the EDIFACT community easily would recognizes the XML code. However, a number of alternative ways of designing the technical solution exist. For demonstration to the EDIFACT community, keeping close to the EDIFACT structure was considered the best thing to do. From a technical perspective this might not be the optimal solution.

5.3. Third lesson learned: it is time consuming to build an XML solution

The technical design and development of an XML solution is as complicated and time-consuming as that of an EDIFACT solution. What makes the work easier is that the business considerations that underlie the EDIFACT standard can he reused in creating the XML solution and indeed has to be reused. It would be a waste of time and effort to re-do any of the complicated and time-consuming standardization work that was done when the EDIFACT messages were created. It is very important to stress that within this context, XML is nothing but an alternative technical solution to exchange data between businesses. The data are the same and thus the decisions made on what information is needed in, for example, a purchase order are still valid in an XML implementation.

5.4. Fourth lesson learned: cultural traps should be bridged

The cultures of the two technical communities (EDIFACT and XML) are rather different and it actually took some time for both sides to understand the scope and purpose of the project. The creation of the XCAT demo was done in close cooperation between skilled EDIFACT and XML technicians who made it possible to finish the demo in a relatively short period of time. This indicates that new ways of working together are needed in order to obtain the full potential of XML used for EDI.

5.5 Fifth lesson learned: XML is space consuming

On the technical side, it is a fact that the XCAT DTD results in XML files that average three times the size of an EDIFACT message in the demo set-up. This experience is important when designing EDI solutions using XML, in the future. Since the information value is the same in an XML message derived directly from the equivalent EDIFACT message, the network must have adequate bandwidth.

5.6 Sixth lesson learned: it is difficult to name the XML tags

A tag in XML always contains the same attributes. In implementation guidelines for EDIFACT messages, data elements of the same type may contain different code lists.

Since the EDIFACT converter does not validate semantic contents, this is not a problem seen from a converter point of view. The validation is done in the application. However, in XML it is possible to validate semantics by checking attributes. This issue could be resolved by building the tag name from both the segment name and the data element. The consequences are that the XML file will grow even bigger and the DTD structure get quite rigid.

5.7 Seventh lesson learned: XML is an immature technology

XML is still a fairly new, technology. In practice this meant that it was not possible to use XSL to display the XML code as we had hoped. At this time Microsoft Internet Explorer does not support XSL. Rather XML is displayed by converting it to HTML.

5.8 Eighth lesson learned: EDIFACT to XML conversion is a technical issue

As long as there is a one-to-one mapping between EDIFACT and XML, the conversion is a purely technical issue.

Glossary

The following terminology includes information collected from various sources, some of which include a general, rather than purely definitive, interpretation.

AEC   Architecture, engineering and construction.

ANSI X12   American national electronic information exchange standard.

API   Application program interface. Allows developers to write programs for a consistent interface to an application program.

application   A specific function or information processing program.

application software Software for a specific use, such as data entry, communications or word processing. Application software runs under the control of systems software.

ASCII	American Standards Code for Information Interchange. Assigns a seven-bit code to 96 printable characters (the characters on an English language keyboard) and 32 control characters. Some codes can have different print/view characteristics with different printers and operating systems (e.g. '£' sometimes becomes '#').
bandwidth	Refers to the capacity of a telecommunications link, and is a measure of how fast data can be moved around. It is measured in cycles per second (hertz, Hz; megahertz, MHz). The greater the number of hertz the wider the bandwidth and the more data that can pass down a channel at any one time.
BMF	Builders' Merchants Federation.
CAD	Computer-aided design. CAD software used by graphic designers, draughtsman and other professional services to draw plans, views, etc.
CITE	Construction Industry Trading Electronically. An electronic information exchange initiative operated by the UK construction industry.
client server	A network system in which one computer acts as a central repository for files and programs that can be shared by a number of client PCs connected to the network.
CSV	Comma-separated value file. A data format used to structure database type information that uses 'commas' as separators between adjacent data elements.
data element	The basic unit of information in an electronic exchange standard. It may be a single-character code, a literal description or a numeric value. Examples of a data element are price, product code, and product attributes such as size or colour.
data segment	Group of well-defined data elements. Typical segments could be 'reference', 'name and address' or 'price' information.

digital certificate (Dcert)	Electronic certificate that can be used to convey a defined level of authorization (e.g. an ordering limit or payment guarantee) in support of an electronic message. These are controlled and provided by 'issuing bodies' who share the responsibility should misuse occur, rather like using a cheque guarantee card to support a payment.
digital signature (Dsig)	A character string designed to prevent possible forgery which is used as a security feature when attached to an electronic message. Can be used to verify the identity of the sender of an electronic message and may be linked to the document contents so that changes would invalidate the signature. (See also *public/private key cryptography*)
EAN	European Article Numbering. Internationally based, unique product, location, etc., numbering system (e.g. as used in product bar codes).
e-business	Electronic business. Often interchanged with e-commerce but which is intended to describe the broader use and impact of electronic information exchange on the entire business process.
e-commerce	Electronic commerce. Transacting business via electronic means. This includes all forms of electronic media but is increasingly used to define buying and selling goods and services using the Internet.
EDI	Electronic data interchange. The electronic transfer of business information from one independent computer application to another independent computer application, using agreed standards to structure the data.
EDIFACT (or UN/EDIFACT)	Electronic Data Interchange for Administration, Commerce and Transport. The international information exchange standards sponsored by the United Nations. Typical examples would be INVOIC (invoice exchange) or DESADV (despatch advice).

EDI software	Software used to manage the exchange of electronic data interchange. Functions include checking message integrity, creating the electronic envelope, sending and receiving messages to/from a value added network (VAN).
EDM	Electronic document management. EDM software applications store documents in electronic format (native files, scanned images, etc.) within a managed environment to support activities such as archiving, retrieval, amendment and distribution.
EIE	Electronic information exchange. A general term used in this book (and elsewhere) to cover the whole spectrum of business applications that involve the transfer of information electronically between computer systems. This term has been adopted to avoid the problems caused by limiting interpretations that have been applied to terms such as EDI, e-commerce, etc.
electronic business	See *e-business*.
electronic commerce	See *e-commerce*.
electronic data interchange	See *EDI*.
electronic document management	See *EDM*.
electronic information exchange	See *EIE*.
e-mail	Electronic mail. The electronic transmission of correspondence from one computer to another. It is possible to send an e-mail with attached computer files (e.g. word processor documents).
encryption	Process of transforming data into a secure format that isn't readable without an electronic key.

ERP	Enterprise resource planning. ERP software comprises business applications that centralize and manage all enterprise information.
extranet	A privately operated 'mini-Internet' that can be accessed externally, i.e. by trading partners. (See also *intranet*)
flat file	File format in which the data are laid out as a string of field values. In the case of the CITE initiative, the flat file adopted used fixed length fields.
FM	Facilities management.
FTP	File transfer protocol. A service providing a family of commands for performing file and directory operations over a network.
functional acknowledgement	Acknowledgement sent back automatically by the receiving application to trading partner on receipt of an electronic message.
gateway	A technical means by which users of one computer system can access another without a separate connection.
GUI	Graphical user interface. The graphically based interface between an application and the operator, commonly applied to operating systems.
hash total	The sum of values for a specific data element.
HTML	Hypertext markup language. An authoring language used for creating documents, especially with Web pages, based primarily on visual appearance.
HTTP	Hypertext transfer protocol. The standard way of transmitting HTML encoded documents over the Internet.
hypertext	The use of direct links from images or phrases in a computer-based document to related text, images, sounds or other data.

IAI	International Alliance for Interoperability. An international, construction industry-based initiative to define 'industry foundation classes', which are implementable data templates that are used to define objects (e.g. a door). These definitions can then be exchanged between applications such as CAD, procurement and specification systems, and be enriched by additional attribute data. Based on the same basic rules as the STEP standards. (See also *STEP*)
ICT	Information and communications technology.
IT	Information technology.
interchange	A group of documents exchanged as a unit between two trading partners.
interchange agreement	A document, usually in the form of a user manual which is adopted by each trading partner, that describes operational, organizational and security requirements relating to the exchange of electronic information.
interchange ID	Identifier used by you and your trading partner or network when sending or receiving electronic data to determine to whom documents are to be routed.
interconnection	The linking of two or more data transfer networks so that messages can be routed between users connected to different network services.
Internet	The worldwide network of interconnected computer systems.
Internet protocol (IP)	The standard that defines the transmission and structure of data sent through the Internet.
intranet	A privately operated 'mini-Internet' facility that uses Internet protocols to provide access to information services, normally within a single organization.
International Organization for Standardization (ISO)	A body to set worldwide communications standards. It has developed the Open Systems Interconnect (OSI) standards and controls some of the data values (e.g. The EDIFACT Unit of Measure codes) used in electronic exchange. The British Standards Institution (BSI) is the UK body within the ISO federation.

IP address	The address of an Internet network interface. (See also *Internet protocol*)
IS	Information systems. General term, sometimes specifically used to define the department responsible for designing office automation resources (computer systems) required to support a company's business processes.
ISDN	Integrated services digital network. A telecommunications service that turns a copper phone line into a high-speed digital link to transmit voice, video images and other data simultaneously.
ISO	See *International Organization for Standardization*.
ISP	Internet service provider.
Java	A computer programming language that works on any platform (i.e. type of computer).
JPEG	Joint Photographic Experts Group. The consortium of hardware, software and publishing interests dedicated to developing international standards for the compression of still photographic images in digital form.
kilobyte (kb or k)	Roughly 1000 bytes. Precisely 1024 bytes. A measure of memory capacity on a computer or the size of a file.
kilocharacter	1000 alphanumeric characters. A unit of measure that is sometimes used for data exchange charging purposes.
LAN	Local area network. A link-up through a central control unit so users in an office, building or locality may share programs, information and other equipment such as modems, printers and plotters. (Compare *WAN*)
leased line	A dedicated circuit, typically supported by a telephone company or transmission authority, that permanently connects two or more user locations and which is for the sole use of the subscriber.
mailbox	Where a third party's computer stores data for a computer which is to receive data.

mapping	In electronic data exchange terms, this is a data-format conversion process that identifies the relationship between one data structure (e.g. an EDIFACT exchange standard) and either an intermediate software interface format (e.g. a flat file) or the application database field(s).
MERNET	An electronic trading initiative established by the Builders' Merchants Federation.
message	A structured exchange of data or a set of information elements transmitted in accordance with agreed rules, to enable a specific business or administrative function.
MIME	Multipurpose Internet mail extensions. A standard for e-mail which enables transfer in any format including binary files, spreadsheets, word processed documents, etc., and graphical information.
MIS	Management information system. Computer applications that provide information to assist managers in decision making or process tracking.
modem	Modulator/demodulator. Modems convert digital data for transmission over telephone lines, but transmit data far more slowly than using ISDN.
MPEG	Motion Picture Experts Group. A consortium of hardware, software and publishing interests dedicated to developing international standards for the compression of moving video images in digital form.
ODETTE	Organization for Data Exchange by Tele Transmissions. An electronic information exchange standard developed within the European automotive industry.
operating system	The program that organizes and manages the activities of a computer and its peripherals, e.g. Microsoft Windows.
procedure	The collection, presentation, communication and processing of data in paper or electronic format.
proprietary format	Data format specific to a company, industry or other limited group. Proprietary formats do not comply with EDI standards.

protocol	Protocols represent the mechanisms that enable hardware, software and communication systems (e.g. a network) to talk to each other.
PSN	Packet switched network. A data communications network where data are divided into small segments, known as packets, in such a manner that each can be independently routed to its destination through a switching network. (See also X25)
PSTN	Public switched telephone network. The term 'public' relates to the customer rather than to the owner.
public/private key cryptography	A method of encryption and decryption in which the sender and receiver each generate a public and private key pair. They exchange and publish the public key (see below). (See also *digital signature*)
	Private key: the key that is never exchanged between trading partners.
	Public key: the key that is exchanged between the trading partners and published.
qualifier	A data element that gives a related segment or data element a specific meaning.
RFID	Radiofrequency identification tag. A tag attached to a product that 'communicates' information carried on it to a base station, using radio waves.
router	Bridge between dissimilar computer networks.
security (electronic)	Process of system screening that denies unauthorized access to application programs and data.
segment	See *data segment*.
SGML	Standard generalized markup language. An ISO standard (8879) for the representation of data structures and relationships. Often associated with text and publishing.
SITPRO	The Simpler Trade Procedures Board. A UK-based organization whose mission is to improve the competitive position of the UK traders by facilitating change, including through electronic trading.

SME	Small to medium sized enterprise. Strict definitions based on turnover, etc., can be misleading. Typically used to define the large number of 'smaller' businesses that exist within a sector (e.g. construction) as distinct from the smaller number of large/dominant organizations.
S/MIME	Secure/multipurpose Internet mail extensions. S/MIME is a specification for secure electronic mail. It uses digital signatures and encryption to add security to e-mail messages in format. (See also *MIME*)
Stand-alone PC	PC class machine that isn't networked to any other computers.
STEP	The Standards for the Exchange of Product Model Data. Based on the Express-G language, STEP standards provide the data templates by which objects can be defined. (See also *IAI*)
syntax	Arrangement of elements in a computer language. Grammar or rules which define the structure of EDI standards.
systems software	Programs that control the internal operation of a computer. They consist of the operating system and packages to improve the efficiency and capabilities of the computer, such as communications control programs and database management programs. Applications software runs under systems software.
TCP/IP	Transmission control protocol/Internet protocol. TCP/IP is a set of communication protocols that support direct communications links with local or wide area networks, including e-mail.
Tradacoms	UK electronic trading standards, used especially within the retail industry. Predates the international EDIFACT standards but continues to be used within sectors of the UK.
translation	The act of accepting documents in other than standard format and translating them to the appropriate standard.
UN/EDIFACT	See *EDIFACT*.

URL	Universal resource locator. An Internet World Wide Web site address.
value added data service (VADS)	An electronic exchange service based upon a mailbox system to enable interworking between a number of organizations. In common usage, this term is frequently used interchangeably with the 'value added network' (VAN).
value added network (VAN)	A service operated by a third party which stores data for other companies that are allowed to either transmit data to the VAN's computers or receive data from them. VANs can also store messages and provide audit information if required.
VPN	Virtual private network. The provision of services normally associated with a private telecommunications network over the shared lines, exchanges and switches of a public network.
WAN	Wide area network. A computer network covering a wide geographical area, e.g. linking the computers of a company with offices in different countries. (Compare *LAN*)
WIPO	World Intellectual Property Association. Part of the United Nations.
World Wide Web	An Internet system that uses hypertext to provide a graphical user interface and links between remote network servers across the Internet, and accessed using browser software.
WWW, Web	See *World Wide Web*.
X25	An international recommendation defining a standard for the software interface and protocols to be used between a data communications network over which data are carried as packets and data terminal equipment. (See also *PSN*)
XML	Extensible markup language. A language designed to support the transfer of structured data within SGML and HTML environments. Particularly relevant to Internet/Web-based applications.

XSL Extensible stylesheet language. A language used in conjuction with XML-based information to manage the visual data interface on a Web browser.

References

1. Goldratt, E. and Cox, J. (1993). *The Goal: A Process of Ongoing Improvement.* Gower, Aldershot.
2. Handy, C. (1990). *Understanding Organizations.* Penguin, Harmondworth.
3. Foster, R. N. (1987). *Innovation, The Attacker's Advantage.* Pan, London.
4. Bicknell, D. (1998). E-commerce barriers – hurdles to be tackled. *Computer Weekly,* 2 July.
5. The Henley Centre/EMAP Construct (19??). *The Future of the Construction Industry – Leading the Change,* section 2.3.5/2.3.6, p. 6.
6. Novis, C. (1997). *EDICON Newsletter,* April.
7. ECQ (1999). Tiles of the unexpected. *eCentre*[UK] *Magazine,* March, p. 4.
8. ECQ (1999). Improving the customer connection. *eCentre*[UK] *Magazine,* March, p. 4.

9. Reckitt & Colman (1998). *eCentre^{UK} (ANA) Case Study 10.*

10. ANA case study. *Johnsons News*, Feb. 1998 (supplied by eCentre^{UK}).

11. The following two items were written by the author with input from several members of the CITE initiative under a DETR project to provide case studies that demonstrated the benefits of IT in construction. The project was managed by the Building Centre Trust and final case studies were published by Construction Research Communications (CRC) Ltd under copyright.

   (a) Cole, T. *Electronic Tendering Case Study.* With special thanks to Andrew Scoones (Building Centre Trust), Charles Brand Associates, C. E. Ball & Partners, DoE Water Service, E. C. Harris and Kvaerner.

   (b) Cole, T. and Oatley, D. *Electronic Invoicing Case Study.* With special thanks to Blue Circle Cement.

12. New South Wales Department of Public Works (1998). *Information Technology in Construction – Making IT Happen.*

13. New South Wales Department of Public Works (1998). *Information Technology in Construction – Making IT Happen* (Summary version).

14. Stark, H. (1997). The Internet: 50% Innovation, 50% Limitation. *Electronic Commerce & Communications*, **2**, No. 10, Nov./Dec.

15. Ford, A. (1997). The Web encourages EDI growth. *Electronic Commerce & Communications*, **2**, No. 8, Sept.

16 Retail perspective: EDI. *Webmaster*, **22**, Aug. 1997.

17. Danish EDI Council, Fischer & Lorenz, Uniware Denmark and Systematic Software Engineering. *XCAT Project.*

18. The Henley Centre/EMAP Construct (1997). *The Future of the Construction Industry.* Section 2.1, p. 4

19. Malcolm, I. (1997). Presentation to the Electronic Commerce Association (now eCentre^{uk}) Financial Interest Section.

20. Malcolm, I. (1997). Financial EDI presentation made to the Electronic Commerce Association (now eCentre) Financial Interest Section.

21. Fox, M. S. *Enterprise Integration*. University of Toronto.
22. The Henley Centre/EMAP Construct (1997).*The Future of the Construction Industry*. Section 3.3, p. 10
23. Till, R. (1999). Submission document by e Centre[uk] and its members to the Trade and Industry Committee inquiry on electronic commerce, Jan.

Index